The Conner Prairie® Cookbook

Edited by Margaret A. Hoffman

Hoosier Hearthside Cookery Series

Conner Prairie Press™
13400 Allisonville Rd
Noblesville, IN 46060

and

Guild Press of Indiana
6000 Sunset Lane
Indianapolis, Indiana 46208

THE CONNER PRAIRIE® COOKBOOK

Edited by Margaret A. Hoffman

 Co-published in the United States by Conner Prairie Press, a division of Conner Prairie, 13400 Allisonville Road, Noblesville, Indiana 46060 and Guild Press of Indiana.

LIBRARY OF CONGRESS CATALOG CARD NUMBER

ISBN 0-9614736-0-6

MANUFACTURED IN
THE UNITED STATES OF AMERICA
First Edition
April 1985
Second Edition, Revised
May 1990

Photography by McGuire Studio, Inc.

Photograph of Mrs. Fenton courtesy *Outdoor Indiana*.

Welcome to the World of Hoosier Hearthside Cookery

The pioneer period of Indiana's settlement (1800-1840) was filled with the perils and pleasures of homesteading in the woods. It was also the time of development of the unique culinary style called "Hoosier cooking."

Indiana was settled largely from the South, from Kentucky and the Carolinas, but other sections were generously represented in the early villages of the Hoosier state. Settlers flat-boated down the Ohio from the East and pioneers came across the National Road from states such as Pennsylvania and New York. New Englanders brought recipes for such things as chowder, pumpkin pie, dandelion wine, and scalloped oysters; Pennsylvania Dutch contributed scrapple and sausage and cabbage recipes. Southerners shared "receipts" for "barbicue," yams and apples and corn pudding.

There was as much diversity among the recipes as there was among the settlers themselves. Elegant dishes such as dressed duck, oyster pie and candied flowers might be found frequently on the table of the richest folk in each settlement, but they also would be found on the groaning boards of the humbler citizens at festive collation or wedding times. And even the wealthiest citizens in a town or on a farm depended on standard dishes such as beefsteak pie, stewed rabbit and chicken, pickles and kraut, batter bread with home-churned butter, and pie plant with custard for everyday meals.

The best way to describe the cookery from Indiana's pioneer period, most of it done right at the fireplace, is to say it is savory, succulent and simple. Taste was a high priority and fresh, easily attainable fruits of countryside and garden predominated.

This cookbook, Volume II in the Hoosier Hearthside Cookery series, presents a potpourri of "receipts" from the 1830s (or thereabouts). They have been developed with the assistance of Margaret Hoffman, long-time interpreter and cooking consultant at Conner Prairie, and adapted for the modern kitchen. They represent years of research by the staff of Conner Prairie and an equal number of years of cooking on the hearth by the museum's excellent cooks.

Most of the recipes here preserve the historic character of much earlier originals by maintaining historic style, language and spelling.

Polly Jontz, Executive Director of Conner Prairie, invites all who love good food to this delectable celebration of Hoosier cookery: "Conner Prairie is pleased to offer this collection of recipes so that you can recreate a few of the memories of good cooking, and a less hurried time, in your own home."

Guild Press of Indiana

Conner Prairie

John and William Conner were two brothers who came into Indiana as traders and Indian interpreters in the first years of the nineteenth century. John Conner became a leading pioneer and member of the first state legislature at Connersville, which is named after him. William Conner established a trading post with the Delaware Indians in central Indiana on the White River. In 1823 he built a distinctive Federal-style house which became a center for a developing pioneer community on the prairie lands around him.

The richly historical house and its acres passed through several hands after his death until it was bought and restored by the philanthropist Eli Lilly, who donated it to Earlham College in 1964. Conner Prairie is now a nationally recognized museum on 250 acres of land, with thirty-seven buildings in its historic area. A modern museum center with a variety of educational and public meeting facilities was opened in 1988.

A storyline has been developed for each of the buildings in the historic area village. This imaginary history, based on detailed research, personalizes the history of the period around 1836 for the thousands of visitors who come to experience pioneer life at Conner Prairie. Costumed interpreters portray the roles of the blacksmith, storekeeper, school teacher, innkeeper and other residents of the "1836 Village of Prairietown." Their imaginary stories form the introductions to each chapter in this cookbook.

Special events are held throughout the year: typical are the spring wedding, summer Independence Day celebration and fall funeral. In December, candlelight tours and winter hearthside suppers allow visitors to sample early Hoosier village life firsthand.

John Schippers
77

CONNER HOUSE

CONNER PRAIRIE COOKBOOK

In 1802 William Conner established a trading post at a fork on the White River, 20 miles north of the present-day city of Indianapolis. The Delaware Indians trusted Conner and traded their furs and pelts at his post, which became known as "Conner's Prairie."

After the signing of the Treaty of St. Mary's, the Delaware Indian tribe moved westward. Conner married Elizabeth Chapman, and in 1823 he replaced his log cabin with a brick house overlooking his vast "prairie." This was one of the first brick houses built in the area and it served as the first post office in the county.

Conner soon became involved in land development and politics, and through the years many guests were invited to share the savory delights cooked in Conner's well-equipped kitchen.

The most impressive of all objects in the Conner kitchen is the huge fireplace with its beehive oven and a clockwork jack that turns the spit. The bricks inside the oven are laid in the shape of a beehive. Two pairs of andirons sit in the fireplace; one pair is used to hold up the fire so hot coals can be removed to the hearth when using a "spider pan" or dutch oven to cook, or when using a trivet. The second pair are called cooking andirons and are built with hooks that support the spit. The clockwork jack is attached to the spit by a long circular chain and is turned by weights.

This "modern" kitchen of the 1820s has served many delicious meals through the years and is a favorite of Conner Prairie's cooks.

ONION SOUP

2 large sweet onions
1 quart milk
½ tsp. mace
½ C. butter
1½ tsp. salt
1 egg yolk
chopped parsley

Thinly slice onions and place in a kettle with milk, mace, butter and salt. Bring to a boil. Cook slowly until the onions are very tender. Pick out the mace blades and discard. Beat the egg yolk in a small bowl and add to it a little of the hot soup, beating constantly. Pour the egg mixture into the hot soup and cook to thicken slightly. Sprinkle each serving lightly with chopped parsley and serve hot.

ANOTHER GOOD ONION SOUP

1 C. butter
10 onions
2 T. flour
4 C. boiling water or beef broth
1 large piece of French bread
salt and pepper to taste
1 egg yolk
1 tsp. vinegar

Heat the butter in a kettle or pan until it bubbles. Peel and chop the onions and put in kettle. Add flour and stir well to blend. Pour in water or beef stock. Add piece of French bread. Put in salt and pepper and stew for 10 minutes. Beat the egg yolk with the vinegar. Mix a small amount of the hot stock with the egg yolk in a small bowl and beat. Pour the egg/vinegar mixture back into the hot stock, stirring gradually to thicken. Serve in a tureen.

PUMPKIN SOUP

½ C. onions
3 T. butter
2 C. mashed pumpkin
1 tsp. salt
1 T. sugar
¼ tsp. ground nutmeg
¼ tsp. ground pepper
3 C. chicken broth
½ C. light cream

Chop the onions and gently brown in the butter in a pan or kettle. Put mashed pumpkin into onions in pan with the salt, sugar, nutmeg and pepper. Slowly add nicely strained chicken broth and heat through. To serve, pour into a tureen and add the cream. Make sure your soup does not boil.

WINTER SOUP

1 bone from roasted leg of lamb
3 quarts water
4 carrots
2 potatoes
2 turnips
2 onions
1 C. dried peas
1 T. salt
1 tsp. pepper
1/2 tsp. thyme
1 tsp. rosemary
1 bay leaf

Put the bone (with some meat still attached)in the soup kettle and cover with water. Put in vegetables, peeled and cut up, with the peas. Add the salt, pepper and herbs with the bay leaf. Cook slowly for an hour. Remove the bone and put back any pieces of meat. Send to the table hot.

BREAD FOR A BEEHIVE OVEN

4 C. scalded milk
4 T. lard
2 T. yeast
1 C. warm water
4 T. sugar
5 tsp. salt
12 C. flour, divided
handful of cornmeal

Add lard to milk and scald in a pan over medium heat. In a good size bowl, melt the yeast in the warm water. While the milk is cooling, put the sugar, salt and flour into your breadmixing bowl, keeping out 2 cups of flour. Mix the cooled milk and yeast and beat into the flour mixture. Knead the bread gradually with the rest of the flour, adding more if needed, until the dough is very smooth. Let rise to double. Punch down, divide and knead again. Shape into four round loaves, this time letting it rise on a board dusted with cornmeal. When doubled, bake in a quick oven (400 degrees) to a golden brown (about 30-40 minutes). Note: If using sour milk, add 2 scant teaspoons of soda.

HOOSIER BISCUIT

1 pint milk
1 tsp. salt
3-4 C. flour
2 T. yeast
1 tsp. cream of tartar
2 T. hot water
2-3 eggs

Add a tablespoon of salt to a pint of new milk, warm from the cow. Stir in flour until it becomes a stiff batter, add two great spoonsful of lively brewer's yeast, put it in a warm place and let it rise as much as it will. When well raised, stir in a teaspoon of saleratus dissolved in the hot water. Beat up three eggs (two will answer), stir with the batter, and add flour until it becomes a tolerable stiff dough. Knead it thoroughly, set it by the fire until it begins to rise, and then roll out, cut to biscuit form, put it in pans, cover it over with a thick cloth, set by the fire until it rises again, then bake in a quick oven (400 degrees) for about 30 minutes, or until golden brown.

A large spoonful of vinegar will sour a cup of milk, if you do not happen to have soured milk on hand. Just let the milk set a bit and pretty soon it will clabber.

SUGAR CAKE

1 C. hot, dry mashed potatoes, unseasoned
1 C. white sugar
3/4 tsp. salt
1 cake yeast, softened in 1 C. warm water
1/2 C. melted butter
1/4 C. lard
2 beaten eggs
4 C. flour, unsifted

Topping:
1/4 pound butter, cut into small pieces
brown sugar and cinnamon

Mash the sugar into the hot potatoes until the sugar melts. Add everything else except the topping mixture. Stir well after each addition. Cover the pan with a warm tea towel and let rise for 5 hours in a warm place. Spoon the batter into 2 pie tins or a turk's head mold. Let rise until puffy.

Topping: Punch holes about an inch apart in the dough and put in the holes one-fourth pound of cold butter chips. Push down the butter chips with a pound of light brown sugar lumps, saving some to sprinkle on top with the cinnamon. Lightly grease the pan, pour in the batter and bake about 25 minutes in a moderate (350-375 degree) oven. Let cool about 5 minutes in pan(s) before turning out on a rack.

WAFFLES

4 C. flour
1 tsp. salt
3 T. yeast
1 quart warm milk
1 T. melted butter
2 eggs

Take a quart of flour, put into it a teaspoonful of salt, and three tablespoons of brewer's yeast. Mix it gradually with a quart of warm milk, having in it a tablespoon of melted butter. Let it rise, and then put two eggs, well beaten, into it. Pour batter onto greased waffle irons and cook until golden brown. Grease the waffle irons well each time they are used.

BEEF STEAK PIE

1 pound lean round steak
salt and pepper to taste
1 tsp. nutmeg
1 onion, sliced
6 cooked potatoes, sliced
3 T. butter
½ C. water
pie pastry for two crusts
½ pint oysters, optional

Butter a large deep dish or pie pan and spread a sheet of pastry all over the bottom. Pepper sides and edge. Cut away from your beef-steak the bone, fat, gristle and skin. Cut the lean in small pieces about as large, generally, as the palm of your hand. Beat the meat well with a rolling pin, to make it juicy and tender. Put a layer of meat over the bottom crust of your dish, season it to your taste with pepper, salt and nutmeg. A small amount of sliced onion is an improvement. Have ready the cold boiled potatoes, slice them thin and spread a layer of them over the meat. Put on a small piece of butter, another layer of meat, then potatoes, and so on until the dish is filled up and heaped in the middle. Pour in the water. Cover the pie with a sheet of pastry and trim and crimp the edges. Notch the top crust several times and bake in a moderate oven (375 degrees) until browned and bubbly, about 45-50 minutes. Oysters may be added to this pie for extra taste.

"The flavor of all herbs is in full perfection just before they begin to blossom: afterwards they begin to decline in sweetness. Gather them on a dry day, cut them into small bunches, and dry them in a slow oven, turning them over frequently. Be careful not to apply too much heat, or the flavor will be too much impaired. When dry, pick off the leaves, powder, sift and cook it up in bottles. It will be found good for flavoring many dishes."
—The Kentucky Housewife, *by Mrs. Lettice Bryan, 1839*

CHICKEN AND OYSTER PIE

3 pound stewing hen
1 quart oysters
½ C. lovage
¾ C. butter
6 T. flour
1 C. chicken broth
1 C. oyster liquor
1 C. cream
salt and pepper to taste
½ tsp. nutmeg
juice of 1 lemon
1 tsp. grated lemon rind
1 receipt pie pastry

Stew the chicken until tender, drain and cool. Drain the oysters and save the liquor. Lightly cook lovage in butter then stir in the flour. Add the broth, liquor and cream and cook until thick. Put in the seasonings. Take the chicken from the bones in large pieces and put into a pudding pan with the oysters. Pour on the sauce. Cover the pie with pastry and moisten the top of the crust with cream. Bake in a moderate oven (375 degrees) until nicely browned, about 45 minutes.

PULLED CHICKEN

Pick all the white meat from the bones of a cold roasted fowl, cut off the legs, and keep the back and sidesmen in one. Score and season the legs with pepper and salt, and broil them; warm up the white meat in some sauce made of the bones boiled in a little water, and which has been strained, and thickened with a piece of butter, mixed with flour and a little milk, and the yolk of an egg beaten up and seasoned with white pepper and salt; serve the broiled back upon the mince, and the legs at each end.

Lovage is an herb whose leaves resemble celery and has the flavor of celery. Substitute celery if lovage is not available.

STEAKS OF MUTTON OR LAMB AND CUCUMBERS

Quarter cucumbers, and lay them in a deep dish, sprinkle them with salt, and pour vinegar over them. Fry the chops in a skillet until a fine (golden) brown, and put them into a stew pan; drain the cucumbers, and put over the steaks; add some sliced onions, pepper, and salt; pour hot water or weak broth on them; stew, skimming off the fat, until chops are tender and done all the way through.

TO BARBICUE A PIG

Scald and clean a pig, of about nine or ten weeks old, the same as for roasting. Make a stuffing with a few sage leaves and the liver of the pig. Put these in a mortar with some bread crumbs, a quarter of a pound of butter, a very little cayenne pepper, and a pint of Madeira wine, beat them to a paste. Sew it up in the pig, lay it at a good distance before a brisk fire, singe it well, put two bottles of Madeira wine into the dripping pan and keep basting it all the time it is roasting. When half done put two French rolls into the dripping pan, and if there is not enough wine in the dripping pan, add more. When the pig is nearly done, take a bunch of sweet herbs and the juice of a lemon, add to the wine in the drip pan. Take up the pig, send it to table with an apple in its mouth, and a roll on each side, then strain the sauce over it.

TO STUFF AND ROAST A CALF'S LIVER

Take a fresh calf's liver, and having made a hole in it with a large knife run in lengthwise, not quite through, have ready a forced meat, or stuffing made of part of the liver parboiled, fat of bacon minced very fine, and sweet herbs powdered, with salt and pepper. With this stuffing fill the hole in the liver. Roll the entire liver well, lay 5-6 strips of fat bacon over the top and then roast, basting occasionally with butter. This is to be served up hot, with gravy sauce having a little wine in it. Bake in a moderate (350 degree) oven until it tests done with a fork.

SPINACH WITH ROSEMARY

2 pounds spinach
1 tsp. parsley
1/4 tsp. fresh rosemary
1 T. green onion
2 T. butter
salt and pepper to taste

Wash the spinach to rid it of all grit and sand. Chop rather fine and place in a kettle with chopped parsley, rosemary and onion. Add the butter, let simmer in its own juice until tender. Remove cover, add salt and pepper.

BRANDIED CRANBERRIES

1 pound fresh cranberries
2 C. brown sugar
1/4 C. brandy

Spread the freshly washed cranberries in an iron spider or heavy skillet. Sprinkle cranberries with the brown sugar, cover and cook slowly for an hour. Remove the lid and pour the brandy over the cranberries. (This may be done in a slack oven after the bread is baked.) You may take it to the table in a pewter basin or for a collation table, in a crystal compote.

PEACHES IN BRANDY

Wipe, weigh, and pick the fruit, and have ready a quarter of the weight of the fruit of fine sugar in fine powder. Put the fruit into an ice-pot that shuts very close, throw the sugar over it (the fruit), and then cover with brandy. Between the top and the cover of the pot, put in a piece of double cap-paper (or brown paper). Set the pot into a sauce pan of water until the brandy be as hot as you can possibly bear to put your finger in, but it must not boil. Put the fruit into a jar, pour the brandy on it. When cold, put a bladder over, and tie it down tight. (Or store in a tight-fitting container.) Serve cold or at room temperature.

APEES

1 C. butter
1⅓ C. sugar
2 eggs
2⅓ C. flour
¼ tsp. cream of tartar
¼ tsp. salt
⅔ C. sour cream

Work the vanilla into the butter and then add the sugar, a little at a time, until it is very smooth. Beat in the eggs. Mix the flour, cream of tartar and salt and add alternately with the sour cream. Drop by spoonsful into baking pans. Bake about 10 minutes in a moderate (350 degree) oven. Cookies should be very pale.

CHEESE PIE

Pastry:
1½ C. flour
½ C. butter
1 large egg
1 T. cold water

Make a rich pastry of the butter and flour. When well mixed add the egg and water. Roll out into a thin circle. Put in a pie dish, trimming edges. Cut nicely (or prick all over with a fork) and bake in a moderate (375 degree) oven for 8-10 minutes.

Filling:
24 oz. cream or cottage cheese
½ C. butter
¾ C. sugar
3 large eggs
1 tsp. nutmeg
2 T. rose water*

*If rose water is not available, you may substitute vanilla extract.

Beat the cheese with the sweet butter. Gradually beat in the sugar and eggs. Put in the nutmeg and flavor, pour in the baked pastry and bake until the custard is set, or 30-35 minutes in a moderate (375 degree) oven.

MAIDS OF HONOR

- 1/2 C. butter
- 1/2 tsp. salt
- 1 C. sugar
- 2 eggs
- 1 1/2 C. flour
- 2 tsp. of baking powder
- 2/3 C. milk
- pie pastry
- apple jelly

Make a cake batter. First, mix the butter and sugar until fluffy, then add the eggs and vanilla. Mix the baking powder with the flour and add to the butter mixture every other time with the milk. Beat very well. Line muffin tins with the pastry, put drop of jelly in, drop in cake batter to make it about 3/4 full. Bake in a moderate (350 degree) oven for about 20 minutes or until cake tests done.

PETTICOAT TAILS

- 5 C. flour
- 1 C. powdered sugar
- 2 C. butter

Mix the flour with the powdered sugar and butter. Shape into rolls and when sufficiently cold, cut into slices and bake in an afternoon (300 degree) oven until edges are lightly brown, 8 to 10 minutes.

> *"An experienced cook knows the value of the articles submitted to her care; and she knows how to turn many things to account, which a person unacquainted with cooking would throw away."*
> —The Housekeeper's Book, *By A Lady, 1837*

PASTRY

¼ pound lard
2 C. flour
1 tsp. salt
⅓ C. ice water

Cut the lard with the salt into the flour until it resembles coarse meal. Add the water and mix rapidly until it is smooth and can be rolled. Do not handle any more than necessary. (The heat from your hands will start the glutton in the flour to working and will make your crust tough.)

PASTRY—OLD RECEIPT

For ordinary purposes half the weight of lard is sufficient but in the richest crusts the quantity should never exceed the weight of flour. Use no more water or other liquid in making paste than is necessary taking care not to put out the Millers eye, that is that the paste will be too moist. The great thing is to incorporate the flour well with the fat, which you cannot do if you allow too much water in the first instance. The under or side crust which should be thin should not be made so rich as the top crust as otherwise it will make the gravy or syrup greasy.

PINE TREE SHILLINGS

1 C. molasses
½ C. butter
½ C. brown sugar
3 C. flour
½ tsp. soda
½ tsp. salt
½ tsp. ginger
1 tsp. cinnamon

Melt together the molasses and butter. In another bowl work together the brown sugar, soda, salt, flour, ginger and cinnamon. Mix both together, make two rolls and get cold. Slice thin and bake in a moderate (350 degree) oven for about 8-10 minutes.

Most folks don't have a shilling in their possession anymore but if you have one you can press the coin into the cookie to make a pine tree impression.

WHITE COOKIES

1 pound fine powdered sugar
1/2 pound butter
4 eggs
1/8 tsp. nutmeg
1/4 tsp. cinnamon
1 jigger of brandy
1 pound sugar

Mix it altogether. Roll thin and cut into shapes. Bake about 8-10 minutes in a moderate (350 degree) oven.

HOT SPICED CIDER

1 quart apple cider
3 cinnamon sticks
4 T. lemon juice
1 tsp. nutmeg
1 tsp. whole cloves

Tie nutmeg and cloves in a small bag of cheesecloth. Mix cider, cinnamon sticks and lemon juice, put in pan (not iron kettle) and simmer a quarter of an hour. Put in spices and simmer to your taste.

"A few things well ordered will never fail to give a greater appetite, and pleasure to your guest, than a crowded table badly prepared; and as there is a time for all things, there will be a time to crowd your table with delicacies."
—The Kentucky Housewife, *by* Mrs. Lettice Bryan, *1839*

McCLURE HOUSE

In 1825, at age 19, Hannah Jane Baldwin became the wife of widower Daniel McClure and the stepmother of Ada Noreen, Silas and Jeremy. To this union were born four children, David and Andrew, living, and Suzannah, stillborn. Another child, John Michael, departed this world after contracting lung fever during the family's first winter in the village of Prairietown.

Mrs. McClure was born to farming parents and had never known any other life until Daniel made the decision to sell his farm and move his family into town. There he realized his ambition and became a carpenter for hire. His wife, worried about feeding her family, hastily planted her garden in the little space available and set about raising what food she could for her family.

To secure what other food supplies they need, Daniel trades his wares to Mr. Whitaker at the store. Mrs. McClure dries and preserves excess vegetables from her garden so there will be plenty for the winter. When the frost of December sets in, the entire McClure family unites in the task of butchering, curing and smoking fresh meat. Mrs. McClure, illiterate, committed her mother's receipt for making sausage meat to memory and Daniel recorded it. Ada Noreen is called upon to make the sausage. Her Pa reads the receipt to her—Daniel sees no reason for book-learnin' for girls!

BEEF SOUP

- 1/4 C. butter
- 2 C. chopped potatoes
- 1 C. water
- 2 T. chopped onion
- 1 T. flour
- 4 C. milk
- 2 C. shredded dried beef
- 2 C. corn
- salt and pepper to taste

Melt the butter in your kettle and add potatoes, onions and the water. Cover and cook until vegetables are tender. Stir in the flour and cook for a minute, then add the milk. Keep stirring. Add shredded beef and corn. Heat but do not boil. Put in salt and pepper.

CORN BREAD

1½ C. flour
1½ C. cornmeal
¼ C. sugar
3 tsp. baking powder
2 eggs
1 C. milk
a little salt
½ C. melted bacon grease

Measure everything dry into a bowl then add eggs, milk and grease. Pour into iron skillet. Bake in a quick (400 degree) oven until golden and set, about 20 minutes. Butter or other grease may be used, but bacon grease is best.

CRACKLIN' BREAD

1 C. cracklin's
1 C. cornmeal
1 C. flour
1 tsp. baking soda
¾ tsp. salt
1 C. buttermilk
2 beaten eggs
⅓ C. drippings

Mix cornmeal, flour, soda and salt with the buttermilk, eggs and the drippings. Beat until smooth then add the cracklin's. Bake in a spider in a quick (400 degree) oven until done and well browned (about 20-30 minutes). Saving your bacon drippings is good economy.

FRIED SALT PORK

Cut salt pork in thin slices. Pour hot water over it, let stand for two minutes. Drain. Dip the pork slices in two beaten eggs and roll in very dry bread crumbs or flour. Fry in hot lard until very crisp on both sides. Serve with hot fried mush, with a little maple syrup or honey, if palatable.

FRIED SALT PORK WITH APPLES

Fried salt pork and apples is a favorite dish in the country; but it is seldom seen in the city . . . After the pork is fried, some of the fat should be taken out, lest the apples should be oily. Acid apples (such as Jonathon or McIntosh) should be chosen, because they cook more easily; they should be cut in slices, across the whole apple, about twice or three times as thick as a new dollar. Fried 'til tender, and brown on both sides—laid around the pork. If you should have some cold potatoes, slice them and brown them in the same way.

SAUSAGE FORCEMEAT

Fry a half pound of sausage for 10 minutes. Drain off fat and add one-quarter cup of the fat to three cups of bread crumbs. Put the sausage to it with two teaspoons of sage, one teaspoon of salt and a little pepper. Mix with one-half cup of hot water. Use to stuff chicken, beef or pork.

SAUSAGE WITH FRIED APPLES

Core unpared apples and cut into rings about half an inch thick. Shape your sausage meat into balls and fry in a spider over low heat until well done but not crisp. Move to a hot platter and keep warm. In about half an inch of fat, add as many apples rings as will fit in comfortably. Sprinkle lightly with brown sugar and cinnamon and cook, turning frequently, with lid on pan to soften apples, then remove cover and cook a little longer or until rings have a rich glaze. Place on platter with sausages to take to table.

SOUSE

Take off the horny parts of the feet and toes of a pig, and clean the feet, ears and tail very thoroughly; then boil them till the large bones slip out easily from the meat. Pack the meat into a stone jar, with pepper, salt and allspice sprinkled between each layer. Mix some good cider vinegar with the liquor in which it was boiled, in the proportion of one-third vinegar to two-thirds liquor from the meat and fill up the jar. Cover tightly and store until ready to eat.

TO MAKE BEST BACON

To each ham put one ounce of salt-petre, one pint bay salt, one pint molasses, shake together six or eight weeks, or when a large quantity is together, baste them with the liquor each day. When taken out to dry, smoke three weeks with cobs or malt fumes.

TO MAKE SAUSAGE

Mix two pounds of fresh lean pork, coarsely chopped, with one-half tablespoon of dried thyme or sage, a dash of cayenne, three-quarters teaspoon ground black pepper and one teaspoon salt. Mix well with your hands. Divide in half and shape into rolls, wrapping well. Sausage will keep several weeks if kept cold.

TO STEW A RABBIT

Clean and wash one rabbit very well and cut into pieces. Roll the meat in flour and brown in a small amount of lard. Remove meat to cool. To the broth add one-half cup of wine and a cup of water. To this, put into the pot six cut-up carrots and one large onion, cut up. When the vegetables are half cooked, peel and cut up six potatoes and add. One cup of mushrooms is a nice addition. Pull meat from the bones and return to pot with two tablespoons of salt and some pepper. Cook slowly until the flavors are well blended. A little chopped garlic may be added during the stewing.

CORN OYSTERS

Grate young, sweet corn into a dish, and to a pint add one egg, well beaten, a small teacup of flour, half a gill of cream, and a teaspoonful of salt. Mix it well together. Fry it exactly like oysters, dropping it into the hot fat by spoonfuls about the size of an oyster and frying until golden brown.

GINGERBREAD

½ C. butter
1 C. sugar
1 egg
1 C. molasses
1 C. soured milk
1 tsp. soda
1 tsp. ginger
3 C. flour

Mix butter and sugar and beat in the egg. Put in molasses, add soda to sour milk and beat it in. Next comes the ginger and flour. Mix it well. Bake in a greased pan in a moderate (350 degree) oven for about 30-40 minutes or until firm.

PIE PLANT PIE WITH CUSTARD

3 C. rhubarb
1½ C. sugar
3 T. flour
½ tsp. nutmeg
1 T. soft butter
2 eggs
pastry for one pie

Cut your rhubarb in inch long pieces. Line pie dish with pastry and place pie plant in pan. Mix the sugar, flour, nutmeg, butter and eggs. Beat well and pour over pie plant. Add a vented lid or lattice lid and bake about 45 minutes in a moderate (375 degree) oven.

"That all-softening, overpowering knell,
The tocsin of the soul,—the dinner bell."
—Lord Byron, 1788-1824

A TABLEAUX OF LIFE IN THE 1830S AND 1840S

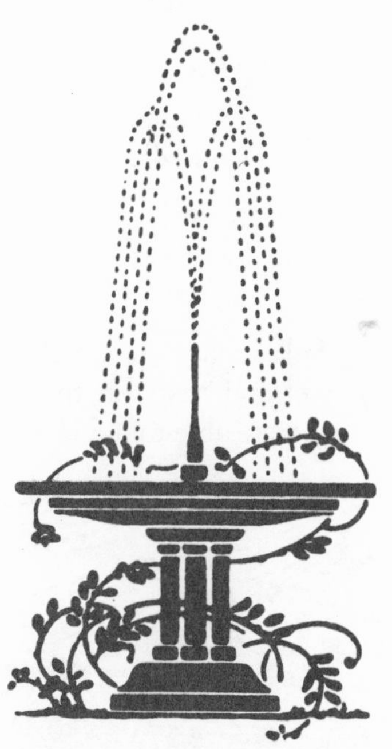

TABLEAUX OF LIFE IN THE 1830S AND 1840S

19th Century Transportation

Getting from "here" to "there" in the 1800s became a lot easier as the years went by. Major developments in transportation occurred in the latter part of the early 1800s, but not all these modes survived.

The first turnpike, built by private companies and financed by private investments and toll revenues, opened as early as 1794 between Lancaster and Philadelphia in Pennsylvania. This successful venture eventually influenced the development of the National Road beginning in 1811. The turnpike eventually faded as a mode of travel primarily for economic reasons.

The canal boom began in the 1810s as a means of connecting existing waterways, and by 1816 there were 100 miles of canals in the country—most, however, were no longer than two miles. Funded by investments, stocks, bonds and direct financing, the United States had more than 3,000 miles of canals by 1840. The boom, however, nearly bankrupted three states, including Indiana, and eventually dropped in popularity.

Railroad development began in the eastern United States during the 1820s and 1830s, and by 1850 there were twice as many railroad miles as there were canal miles.

Flatboats were commonly used until the 1830s, when steamboats began to dominate river travel and trade on the Great Lakes. Steamboats were faster and cheaper and were able to maneuver internal waterway connections.

Indiana Governor Noah Noble (1831-1837), known for his lavish hospitality, was head of the ship of state when it almost foundered during the canal mania, a speculative boom that overspent the state's treasuries.

An 1834 stagecoach crosses between St. Louis and Vincennes in Indiana.

In the 1830s the velocipede was seen on the streets of larger cities such as Indianapolis. Many a daring beau tried to push it with his toes, like a scooter over the bumpy roads.

Ladies dressing using corsets of the 1830s.

Golden Eagle Inn Rates
½ Pint Whiskey, 6¼ cents
Lodging, 12½ cents
Meals, 25 cents
½ Pint Brandy, 6¼ cents
½ Pint Wine, 6¼ cents

Dr. Campbell's General Prescription

Bleed for fevers. Puke for bad stomach. Blister for aches and pain. Purge the bowels for cleansing the system.

Independence Day 19th Century Style

The post-Revolutionary War era of the early 19th century provided the perfect climate for intensely patriotic ceremonies—especially on July 4. Although Independence Day was not an official national holiday in 1836, families and individuals tried to set aside the day as special, reserving it for feasting, celebration and gathering.

The militia, usually an all-volunteer group of local men, would gather and march through the community to the sound of a drum and fife, and someone would have the honor of reading the Declaration of Independence. The reading often was interrupted with shouts of loyalty and patriotism from the crowd.

Impromptu dances would take place when the fiddler struck a tune, and the militia would gather for a friendly competition at the shooting range. Families would cook for days to serve as lavish a feast as possible, augmented by delicious mid-summer garden produce.

The children enjoyed games of ball and quoits and gentlemen rarely avoided the opportunity for a little political debate. The women were busy preparing the noonday feast in the kitchen, although there always was time for a brief dance if it was deemed appropriate.

The day might end as the strains of "Hail Columbia" carried from the center of town through the open windows of rustic log cabins and clapboard-sided homes.

The flag was the symbol of freedom, military glory, and patriotism in a bold, new land.

14 THE CHILD'S PICTURE

THE INDUSTRIOUS BOY.

A good boy.
A grassy bank.
Thick paper.
A lead pencil.
A picture.
A cottage.
Three windows.
One door.
A high tree.
A church.
A high steeple.
A black hat.
A bare head.
A good seat.
A cool place.
A thistle.

This primer from the Conner Prairie collection was an innovation: it helped children learn to spell and read by looking at child-oriented pictures.

School Lessons:

Geography Lesson
East is Ohio's fertile land
And north the tract called Michigan
West Illinois, but south the stream
Of the Ohio may be seen.

Counting Lesson
One, two buckle my shoe
Three, four open the door.
Five, six, pick up the sticks
Seven, eight, lay them straight.
Nine, ten a big fat hen.
Eleven, twelve dig and delve.

Vowels Lesson
ba be bi bo bu
aeiou
ca ce ci co cu
aeiou
da de di do du
aeiuo

"We may live without poetry, music and art;
We may live wthout conscience and live without heart;
But civilized men can not live without cooks."
—Edward Lytton, Earl of Lytton, 1831-1891

Games

From *How to Entertain a Social Party*, author and date unknown, but circa mid-1800s.

TRANSPOSITIONS

A capitol game to sharpen wits and one from which amusement for many hours may be extracted. The company sit round a table (or you can break up into groups,) and each person is provided with a pencil and scrap of paper. Each one writes on his or her scrap a name of a city, country, river, mountain, or if preferred, of some historical or famous personage, transposing the letters so as to make the recognition of the word as difficult as possible, and accompanying it with a few written works of explanation (subtle hints). Then the papers are folded together and deposited in the middle of the table; and when they have been well mixed, a folded paper is drawn by each player and those who cannot decipher the transposition which has fallen to their share are condemned to pay a forfeit. The game begins anew with the remaining players. This process is repeated until a winner is revealed. (There should be a 3 to 5 minute time limit given to decipher the transposition.)

Example:

kubren lihl (Where it is said, "Don't fire until you see the whites of their eyes!") answer: Bunker Hill

dawren kancojs ("One man with courage makes a majority." This person was a general in the War of 1812 and served as President of the United States.) answer: Andrew Jackson

HOW DO YOU LIKE IT? WHERE DO YOU LIKE IT? AND WHEN DO YOU LIKE IT?

This is a guessing game. One of the company retires, while the rest fixes on some article or object—for instance—a light, an apple, money, etc. the person who is out is recalled, and proceeds around the circle, asking each player in succession, "How do you like it?" Supposing the thing thought is money, the first may answer, "In abundance," the second, "Ready," and so on. The questioner tries to gain from the answers thus given some clue to the nature of the thing thought of. The second and third questions are played in the same manner. Someone is almost sure to drop a hint which will set the guesser upon the right track. Three guesses are allowed him. If he succeeds, he must point out the player whose answer gave him the clue, and the latter pays a forfeit and goes out to be puzzled in his turn. Failing to guess in three trials, the first player must try another question. The art of the game consists in choosing words with more meanings than one, such as cord and chord; for then the answers may be varied in a very puzzling manner. One will like his "cord" around his box, while another may like his "chord" in music.

CROSS QUESTIONS AND CROOKED ANSWERS

The company sit round, and each one whispers a question to his neighbor on the right; and then whispers an answer (unrelated) to the person on his left. Then every player has to recite the questions he received from one player and the answer he got from the other, and the ridiculous incongruity of these random cross questions and crooked answers will frequently excite a good deal of sport. For instance one might say, "I was asked what I like for dinner and the answer was, 'The Emperor of China.' "

FASHIONS AND FRIPPERIES

Perfumes

From the *Kitchen Directory*, 1846

Turn a quart of alcohol gradually on to the following oils: a couple drachms of the oil of rosemary, two of the oil of lemon or orange flower water, one drachm of lavender, ten drops of oil of cinnamon, ten of cloves and teaspoon of rosewater. Keep the whole stopped tight in a bottle—shake it up well. It will do to use as soon as made, but it is much improved by age.

From the *American Economical Housekeeper*, 1850

Take two drachms of oil of rosemary, two of oil of lemon, one of lavender, ten of cinnamon, one teaspoonful of rosewater. Pour on these one quart of alcohol; put all in a glass bottle and shake it up well; to have it very clear, put some cotton in a funnel, and place a piece of tissue or printing paper over it, and strain contents through it.

Steaming Herbal Facial

Put two cups of herbs or flowers (lavender, rose buds, peppermint) in a basin. Cover with boiling water. Make a tent for your head with a towel and let the steam wreath your face for about 10 minutes. Interesting variations: add 1 tablespoon crushed fennel seeds. or dried sage.

Honey Water Hand Lotion

- 3/4 cup of Rosewater
- 1/4 cup of Glycerine
- 1/2 t. Vinegar
- 1/2 t. Honey

Mix and blend well by shaking the bottle. Use often for best results.

Luxury Bath Soak

- 7 parts lavender
- 6 parts rosemary
- 5 parts rose petals
- 4 parts lavage leaves
- 3 parts lemon verbena
- 1 part each: thyme, sage, mint, marjoram, orris root

Mix dried herbs together and keep in a closed jar. At bath time, put 1/4 cup of mixture into a square of muslin. Tie it securely. Boil the pouch in a quart of water for about 10 minutes. Add the scented water to your bathtub. Use the muslin ball to scrub with after you have soaked to your heart's content.

Herbal Bathing Vinegar

Select from one or several of the following: lavender, rosemary, peppermint, lemon verbena, rose petal or chamomile. They are good separately or blended. Put two cups of dried herbs into a large (at least a quart size) jar. Heat one quart of good quality white vinegar to a boil and pour it over the herbs. Cover the solution tightly. Twice each day, shake the jar vigorously. After two weeks of this blending, strain the liquid through cheesecloth. Pour it in pretty jars. Decorate the solution with a fresh sprig of the herb, if you like. Bathing vinegar can be added to a tub bath, or used as a sponge bath solution.

Herbal Skin Oil

Use 1 tablespoon of dried sage of rosemary, in 4 oz. of safflower oil (or wheat germ oil). Place in a tightly covered glass jar and store in the refrigerator for 3 or 4 days before using. This can be used for cleansing and is very soothing.

Quick Herbal Rinse

Bring 2 cups water to boil. Add 1 or 2 tablespoons dried sage (for brunettes) or rosemary. Take off heat and steep for 15 minutes. Strain and use as a rinse.

Fashion in the Early 19th Century

Taken from *Men and Women, Dressing the Part*, by Claudia Brush Kidwell and Valerie Steele

A fashionable individual in the 1840s sported the hourglass shape. Not just women, but men donned outfits that featured sloping shoulders, a padded chest and a narrow waist. Beside the obvious differences of skirts and pants, the hourglass look was achieved differently between the two sexes. Women were more likely to use undergarments to construct their fashionable figures—corsets to rearrange their flesh, petticoats and bums, or crescent-shaped bustle pads, to enhance the hips. Their dresses served primarily as an outer covering, cut and trimmed to emphasize the form they had built. Men's fashionable silhouettes, however, were more often built into their clothes by their tailors. It was the skillfully cut and artfully padded coat, vest, and trousers that transformed the average masculine body into the desired hourglass shape.

19th Century Party Dress

Taken from *Letters of Emma Passavant*, 1826

The next evening, therefore, I dressed myself in my white frock, red sash, and one of the girls lent me a little lace to quill around the bosom; Miss

Betsy *herself* fixed my hair and put some flowers out of the glass, which she stuck in my head—a geranium leaf and two rosebuds—I wrapped myself in a cloak and in a moment we were there. I was led into an elegant parlour with folding doors, filled with richly dressed Gentlemen and Ladies, particularly the latter, who were attired in a most elegant manner; almost everyone wore white satin shoes, with pearls, and jewels in the hair, bunches of curls and artificial flowers; satin spencers ornaments with nits lace, thick silk manufactured in the most tasty manner with rouleaus—and I know not what all. Beautiful necklaces of pearl and Topaz, in fact they were almost all tastily and handsomely dressed; even old women wore artificial flowers and such a scene of beauty and fashion, and smiles, and gayety, I had never seen before.

Early 19th Century Parties

Taken from Calvin Fletcher's Diary (New Year's Eve, 1822)

About 3 of the clock, Mr. Hogden called with a carriage and carried Mrs. F. and myself to Mr. Wyant's, on the river where we met about twenty couple. We enjoyed ourselves very much and returned about twelve, and not fatigued. . . The refreshments were elaborate. Rev. J. C. Fletcher records Mrs. Martin's account of them thus: According to Mrs. Martin there was in the great open fire place an immense kettle or cauldron, which contained no less than sixteen gallons of coffee; and there were pans, skillets and other cooking and baking vessel, in which were biscuits, sweet bread, ginger bread, and that best of all cakes which is a lost art among the moderns. . . There was dancing as well as eating. On this occasion, under his inspiring strains Mattias R. Nowland invited Mrs. Wyant to open the dance with him. Others followed, and all was going as merry as a wedding bell when Mr. Wyant entered and ordered the music to stop. According to J. H. B. Nowland: Mr Wyant said that as far as himself and his wife were concerned, they were capable of and able to do their own dancing, and that he thought it would look better for every man to dance with his own wife . . .

Godey's Ladies Book *provided a glimpse of the latest silken gowns from Paris and London beginning in the 1840s, as well as inspiring pieces to help ladies live well at home and in the world. From the Conner Prairie Collection.*

An 1840s Godey's Ladies Book shows the dramatic change in fashions from 10 years earlier. As leisure time became more available at mid-century, more effort could be given to finer dressing.

In the later period fancy bonnets, quilted material and lace accented day dresses.

Some plates in women's magazines of the 1840s were beautifully hand colored in an assembly line print shop.

Notes on Party Etiquette, taken from *A Young Lady's Friend*, written by a lady, 1836

Your hair should be arranged with great neatness and everything about you should be in perfect order; for daylight reveals those little defects which candle-light conceals.

Look towards the lady of the house, and walk up at once to her, not turning to the right or left, or noticing any one, till you have made your courtesy to her, and to the host.

A child, a picture, an annual, a worked ottoman, a bunch of flowers, may furnish topics for conversation till dinner is announced. When that moment comes, stand back for all the married dames to pass out before you.

On entering the dining room, you must use your eyes to discover which part of the table is considered the most honorable; . . . Try to seat yourself among the least important portion of the company. . .

If soup is helped first, take some, whether you like it or not; because, if you do not, you alone may be unemployed . . .

It must depend on the number of servants in attendance, and on the style in which the dinner is given, whether it is proper for you to pass plates or not; at some tables it is a necessary attention, whilst at others it would be a barbarous piece of officiousness.

Leisure Activities

Although women of the 1830s and 1840s had more time for leisure activities than did their mothers and grandmothers, life was still primarily centered around domesticity and child-rearing.

Taken from *The Bonds of Womanhood*, by Nancy F. Cott

By the mid 19th century, the literacy rate had increased dramatically among women. Keeping a diary was considered a leisure activity (mostly to unmarried women).

An 1815 diary entry from Sarah Ripely Stearns, "I do not find so much time to write in my journal as formerly when I lived in my father's house—the cares of a rising family & feeble state of health, take up much time day after day, month after month passes away & I see but little that I have done."

Married women with servants and unmarried women spent their precious few leisure hours with social visits, church and lecture attendance, shopping, walks and charity organizations, dances, language lessons, needlework, painting and reading.

Literary Societies brought women together to discuss current literary work, women's attitudes, values and gossip.

Temperance Meetings were other social gatherings that brought men and women together to support alcoholic abstinence or at least support only its moderate consumption.

Quilting "bees" brought together village women to mix work and social visits.

Traveling religious circuit riders, and religious camp meetings all gave women a break from: ". . . sewing of skirts, gowns and coats—knitting gloves and stockings, baking, brewing, preserving food, churning butter, gardening, nursing the sick, making candles or soap, washing, ironing, scouring . . . "

Tobacco and the use of "spiritous liquors" were common but frowned on. This 1836 illustration shows a surprisingly modern condemnation of smoking for reasons of health.

THE

AMERICAN

FRUGAL HOUSEWIFE.

DEDICATED TO THOSE

WHO ARE NOT ASHAMED OF ECONOMY.

BY MRS. CHILD,

AUTHOR OF "HOBOMOK," "THE MOTHER'S BOOK," EDITOR OF THE "JUVENILE MISCELLANY," &c.

A fat kitchen maketh a lean will.—FRANKLIN.

"Economy is a poor man's revenue; extravagance a rich man's ruin.

TWELFTH EDITION.

ENLARGED AND CORRECTED BY THE AUTHOR.

BOSTON:

CARTER, HENDEE, AND CO.

1833.

The American Frugal Housewife by Mrs. Child was a book "dedicated to those who are not ashamed of economy." Many women publishers of similar books during the time would not have used their names, as it was considered too bold.

MUTTON.

1. Leg.
2. Loin, best end.
3. Do. Chump do.
4. Neck, best do.
5. Do. Scrag do.
6. Shoulder.
7. Breast.
   Saddle, 2 Loins.

PORK.

1. The Sperib.
2. Hand.
3. Belly, or Spring.
4. Fore Loin.
5. Hind do.
6. Leg.

VEAL.

1. Loin, best end.
2. Do. Chump do.
3. Fillet.
4. Knuckle, hind.
5. Do. fore.
6. Neck, best end.
7. Do. scrag do.
8. Blade Bone.
9 Breast, best end.
10. Do. Brisket.

BEEF.

Hind Quarter.

1. Sir Loin.
2. Rump.
3. Aitch Bone.
4. Buttock.
5. Mouse do.
6. Veiny piece.
7. Thick Flank.
8. Thin do.
9. Leg.

Fore Quarter.

10. Fore Rib, 5 Ribs.
11. Middle do. 4 do.
12. Chuck, 3 do.
13. Shoulder, or Leg Mutton piece.
14. Brisket.
15. Clod.
16. Neck, or Sticking piece.
17. Shin.
13. Cheek.

Women, who often participated in butchering, needed to know cuts of beef. They learned them from animal charts such as these found in 19th century cookbooks.

"Indiana is a vast forest, larger than England, just penetrated in places by the backwoods settlers who are half hunters, half farmers. . . . They are the fields of enterprise, the cradle of freedom, the land of rest to the weary, the place of refuge to the oppressed." Elias P. Fordham, c. 1817, "The Old Northwest"

Typical Travel Times (1820-1843)
Noblesville to Indianapolis, 4-6 hours
Indianapolis to Cincinnati, 2 days
Indianapolis to Fort Wayne, 5 days
Philadelphia to Indianapolis, 3 weeks

The Great Migration continued well into the 1830s, with settlers pouring out of the East and South into the new Northwest.

GOLDEN EAGLE INN

Martha Sophia Leaman Zimmerman and her husband, Johan, originally from Pennsylvania, established their first home in Indiana on a farm in eastern Marion County along the Brookville Road. Their home soon became the resting place for weary travelers, drovers and wagoners. One distinguished visitor was Dr. George Washington Campbell who persuaded the Zimmerman family to remove to Prairietown and become proprietors of his newly completed Golden Eagle Inn.

During the cold, rainy season of the fall of 1835, Johan became very ill and succumbed, leaving Mrs. Zimmerman alone. She had to make a decision about her future in Prairietown. It must be said that few women were lone proprietors of such establishments but it was not unusual for a widow to inherit such a position. Dr. Campbell, impressed with her ability, encouraged Martha to undertake the management of the Golden Eagle Inn. Summoning all of her iron-willed German courage, she agreed to assume the authority. The occasional rowdy drover, the campaigning politician or traveling actor who seeks a night's lodging soon learns that Mrs. Zimmerman runs a decent, respectable inn.

With the help of her daughter, Suzannah, Martha Zimmerman serves hearty, savory meals that have become favorites of lodgers and travelers to the new western frontier. A kettle of stewed meat or spicy soup will almost always be bubbling over the fire when visitors stop by to rest after their long journey.

RAISIN SOUP

1 C. raisins
1 onion
3 T. parsley
1 tsp. caraway seed
½ C. lovage
6 C. chicken stock
¼ C. flour
½ C. milk
½ C. sugar
2 T. vinegar

3 eggs yolks, whipped
1 C. sour cream

Soak the raisins in water in a pan to plump them. Add to the raisins finely chopped onion, parsley and lovage. Cook slowly for 20 minutes. Drain. Stir in flour mixed with milk. Cook until thick. Mix chicken stock, sugar and vinegar and put it into milk mixture. Mix the yolks with the sour cream and whisk it in. Keep it warm and take to table. Sufficient for eight.

CABBAGE AND APPLES

2 medium onions
4 T. butter
½ tsp. nutmeg
2 tsp. salt
2 C. water
2 T. vinegar
large head cabbage
4 apples

Chop the onions fine and brown in the butter in a skillet. Add nutmeg, salt and pepper. Cook half an hour with the water and vinegar. Shred the cabbage, pare and slice the apples. Put cabbage and apples in with onions, cover and cook until tender. Enough for eight with a meat dish.

CHICKEN AND NOODLES

2-3 pound chicken
cold water
salt
2½ C. flour
3 eggs
1 tsp. salt

Put a 2-3 pound chicken in a medium size kettle, cover with cold water that is lightly salted and stew the meat until if falls from the bones. Pick out the bones and skin. Strain broth, set meat aside.

Noodles: Put the flour into a bowl, make a hole in the flour, break in the eggs and add the salt. Stir eggs briskly with a fork, gradually working flour in from the outer edges. Make a stiff dough. Divide into two parts and roll very thin, fold and slice very narrow. Bring broth to a rolling boil, pour noodles into the broth all at once, and stir rapidly with a fork to separate noodles. Last, return chicken to broth and spice to taste. Cook until noodles are done.

CHICKEN PIE

double receipt of dough for biscuits
1 chicken
6 potatoes
2 C. peas
marjoram
parsley
2 eggs
light cream

Line the sides but not the bottom of a 3-quart baking pan with part of the biscuit dough. Put in a layer of cooked chicken free of skin and bones. Cover with a layer of raw potatoes, peeled and sliced very thin. Sprinkle on some of the peas with salt and pepper. Lay a few very thin strips of half the remaining dough and sprinkle light cream with chopped marjoram and parsley. Repeat layers until pan is three quarters filled. Mix eggs and cream and pour over. Put on a thick crust, making a slit for steam. Bake in a moderate (350 degree) oven until golden brown (about 45 minutes).

CHICKEN PIE—A DIFFERENT ONE

1 good size chicken
1/4 tsp. saffron
2 large onions
1 dessert spoon salt
6 peppercorns
2 quarts broth

4 large potatoes
4 carrots
parsley, fresh or dried
1 receipt pie squares

Cook the chicken with the onions, chopped, the saffron and salt and peppercorns. Simmer until done and then strain and remove the chicken from the bones. Cut it into small pieces. Put two quarts of broth back into the pot, add the potatoes and carrots, cut into small pieces. When it boils, add the pie squares. Do not cover. Cook until tender. Put the chicken and some parsley back into the kettle and heat well.

HEAD CHEESE

Take the head, feet, ears and tail of a hog, and boil them until every bone falls out. Then take all the meat, both fat and lean, and put into an earthen pan. Season it with salt, pepper, sage, cloves and summer savory, or any spice and herbs you may prefer. Put it into a coarse cloth, twist it up; and lay a stone upon it. This is a very favorite article of food in some parts of the country, and certainly is very good. Great care is necessary in cleaning such giblets of pork. I am unable to say how the water may be used in which the pieces were boiled; but the recent improvements in making glass from pig's feet, as it is made from calves' feet, show that it might be put to good use.

OYSTER FORCEMEAT

1 pound white bread
1 C. butter
1 large onion
1 rib celery
2 tsp. salt
1/4 tsp. pepper
1 quart oysters

Crumble one loaf firm bread. Melt the butter in a skillet and add chopped onion and celery. Cook until of a golden color. Stir into bread crumbs. Add 1/4 C. parsley, chopped, salt and pepper. Drain the liquor from the oysters and heat the liquor to the boiling point. Add the oysters and cook until the edges of the oysters begin to curl. Drain and stir the oysters into stuffing. Makes enough forcemeat to stuff a 12 to 15 pound turkey.

PORK AND KRAUT

1 receipt of dumplings
3-4 pounds pork (pieces)
3-4 T. brown sugar, optional

Cover three or four pounds of pork with water and cook until done to your liking. Put in 2 quarts kraut and cook for about half an hour. Drop in the dumplings and cook with a cover on for 15 minutes without looking. Some like the addition of a little brown sugar.

PORK-HAM LOAF

3/4 C. butter
1 large onion, chopped
1 C. dry bread crumbs
1 C. milk
2 eggs
2 cloves garlic
1/2 tsp. dried thyme
1/4 tsp. pepper
1/4 tsp. cloves
1/4 tsp. marjoram
1/2 C. Madeira wine
1 1/4 C. ground smoked ham
1 3/4 pound ground fresh lean pork

Melt the butter in a skillet and brown the chopped onion. While your onion is cooking, soak the dry bread crumbs in the milk. Stir the chopped onions and soaked bread crumbs together with the beaten eggs, garlic, thyme, pepper, cloves and marjoram. Put in the wine and the pork and ham and mix well. Bake slowly until done in a medium (375 degree) oven. This will take two to three hours. Loaf will be set and browned on top. Cut when cooled. The flavor gets even better after a couple of days.

SCRAPPLE

Take the heart, and any lean scraps of pork, and boil, until it will slip easily from the bones. Remove the fat, gristle, and bones; then chop fine. Set aside the liquor in which the meat was boiled until cold. Take the cake of fat from the surface, and return to the fire. When it boils, put in the chopped meat, and season well with pepper and salt. Let it boil again. Then thicken with cornmeal as you would in making ordinary cornmeal mush. Cook one hour, stirring constantly at first, then putting back on the stove to boil gently. When done, pour in a long pan to mold. This can be kept several weeks in cold weather. Cut in slices and fry brown as you do mush.

TO COOK SAUERKRAUT

Put your kraut into a kettle. Pour boiling hot water over—enough to cover the quantity of kraut you wish to use. Let it boil for three hours, well covered. Some prefer a piece of salt or pickled pork cooked with.

TO STEW MEAT WITH SAUERKRAUT

Cut a pound of bacon from the slab, cut it fine, fry it and remove from pan. Put in four chopped onions a few minutes, put in three pounds of chopped up beef and same of fresh pork, put to it some salt and pepper and cook 'til lightly browned. In another kettle put ten pounds of fresh, washed and drained sauerkraut and boil, then cook slowly for a quarter of an hour. Drain the kraut and put it in a large roasting pan with all the meat and juices. Put in five bay leaves, two small onions that are quartered and a pound of sliced smoked sausage. Mix together and put on top another pound of the sausage. Bake for two or three hours. If too juicy, thicken with four tablespoonsful of flour rubbed into a tablespoonful of butter. Serve it up with boiled potatoes and cold beer. Sufficient for twenty.

CABBAGE CREAMED

Take one pint of cold, cooked cabbage chopped fine and place in a bake-dish. Heat a pint of milk. Melt in a saucepan one tablespoonful of butter and add two tablespoonsful of flour. Stir until mixed well. Then add the hot milk a little bit at a time, stirring 'til smooth for each addition. Add one teaspoonful of salt and a little pepper; pour the milk mixture over the chopped cabbage; melt two tablespoonsful of butter, add eight tablespoonsful of rolled cracker crumbs and sprinkle this over the top of your cabbage. Bake in a moderate (350 degree) oven 'til hot and a delicate brown, about 30-45 minutes.

CABBAGE PUDDING

Get a fine head of cabbage, not too large; pour boiling water on, and cover it till blanched so you can turn the leaves back, which you must do carefully; take some of those in the middle of the head off; chop them fine, and mix them with rich forcemeat; put this in, and replace the leaves to confine the stuffing—tie it in a cloth and boil it—serve it up whole, with a little melted butter in a dish.

FRIED CORN MEAL MUSH

Boil five cups water in kettle. Mix one and one-half cups corn meal with one teaspoon salt and one and a half cups cold water. Stir into boiling water, a little at a time, stirring constantly. Cook over high heat about three minutes. Cover and cook fifteen minutes longer over medium heat. Pour into greased pan and cool. Cut the firm mush into slices. Beat one egg yolk with two tablespoons milk, dip slices in mixture and then coat with fine dry bread crumbs. Fry in heated butter or bacon fat until crisp and golden. Serve hot with warm maple syrup.

FRIED CUCUMBERS

A third part of sliced onion is sometimes fried with cucumber slices in a little butter for a good taste.

FRIED HOMINY

Fry bacon, cut into pieces, and pour off most of the grease. Add hominy and chopped onions, salt and pepper and cook until browned. Use 6-8 strips of bacon to a quart of hominy.

GREEN CORN PUDDING

Cut two cups green corn from cob. Beat three eggs vigorously, then stir in corn and a mixture of one-quarter cup flour, one teaspoon salt, one-half teaspoon pepper, then two tablespoons butter, melted, and two cups light cream. Pour into buttered baking pan, place in spider containing about one and a half inches of water, and bake until a silver knife inserted comes out clean.

SAUERKRAUT

Get your cabbage the last of September, by the hundred. Remove the outer leaves and cores of the cabbage and cut fine with a cabbage cutter. Put down in large (5 gallons) jars. Put a very little sprinkle of salt between each layer, and pound each layer with a wooden masher or mallet. When your vessel is full, place some large cabbage leaves on top, and a double cloth wrung out of cold water. Then a cover with a very heavy weight on it—a large stone is best. Let it set for six weeks before using, being careful to remove the scum that rises every day, by washing out the cloth, the cover and the weight in cold water. After six weeks, pour off the liquid and fill over with clear, cold water. This makes it nice and white. Store covered in a cool place.

DUMPLINGS

For dumplings, mix together two cups of flour with three teaspoons baking powder, one teaspoon salt, three tablespoonsful of melted butter with one cup milk. Drop into boiling pork and sauerkraut. Put on a cover and let cook for fifteen minutes without looking.

DOUGHNUTS

4 C. flour
1/2 tsp. salt
1/2 C. sugar
1 T. dry yeast
1/2 C. butter
1 C. hot milk
lard
sugar

In a large bowl mix the flour, salt,sugar and yeast. In another bowl put the butter and add hot milk to melt. Let cool until just warm. Mix all together and stir to make a thick batter. Cover and let stand to double. Put a good deal of lard in kettle and heat to very hot, stir batter and drop by teaspoon into hot lard. Let the doughnuts rise up, and turn themselves over. Cook until browned. Drain and dust with sugar, if desired. Make the doughnuts very small so that they are cooked through.

> *"The eating too little is hurtful, as well as eating too much. Neither excess, nor hunger, nor anything else that passes the bounds of nature, can be good to man."*
> —The Cook's Own Book, *by a Boston Housekeeper (Mrs. N.K.M. Lee), 1832*

PIE SQUARES

3 T. lard
2 C. flour
½ tsp. salt
½ tsp. soda
¾ tsp. cream of tartar
1 egg
⅓ C. cold water

Mix in order. Roll thin, cut into squares of about 2 inches with a pastry jig or knife. Cook with boiling pork and kraut or other receipts.

RYE BREAD

1½ C. milk
¼ C. honey
1 T. salt
2 T. lard
2 T. yeast
3 C. rye flour
3½ C. white flour

Scald the milk then add the honey, salt and lard and let cool to lukewarm. Put to it the yeast. Now add the rye flour and a cup of the white flour. Now add the other 2½ cups of flour, turn onto a lightly floured board and let rest for ten minutes. Knead with greased hands until smooth and elastic. Turn in greased bowl until covered with grease, cover and let rise to double. Without punching down, turn on to lightly floured board and divide into 2 parts. Shape into two loaves. Place in greased pans and let rise to double. Bake. Brush with butter while hot.

APPLESAUCE

Pare, core and slice some apples, and put them in a stone jar, into a saucepan of water, or on a hot hearth. If on a hearth, let a spoonful or two of water be put in, to hinder them from burning. When they are soft, bruise them by mashing them, and put to them a piece of butter the size of a nutmeg, with a little brown sugar. Serve it in a sauce-tureen.

APPLESAUCE CAKE

2 C. sugar
2 C. flour
1/2 C. lard or butter
1 1/2 tsp. baking powder
1 1/2 tsp. soda
1 1/2 tsp. salt
3/4 tsp. cinnamon
1/2 tsp. cloves
1/2 tsp. allspice
1/2 C. water
2 eggs
1 C. raisins
1/2 C. nuts
1 1/2 C. applesauce

This receipt will make 2 cakes if baked in a 10-inch spider or 10-inch pudding pans. Mix sugar and lard or butter well. In separate bowl, mix flour, baking powder, soda, salt and spices, then add alternately with mixture of water, applesauce and eggs to lard/sugar mixture. Put in raisins and nuts last. Spoon into an 11 x 13 pan. Cook in a medium quick oven (350°) for about 40 minutes. This receipt makes good cookies if more flour is added so batter can be dropped by spoonsful onto baking sheets.

BROWN SUGAR ICING

1 C. brown sugar
1 C. white sugar
1 C. milk
1 T. corn syrup
1 T. butter
pinch of salt

1 tsp. vanilla
¼ tsp. baking powder

Bring the sugars, milk, corn syrup, butter and salt to a boil. Continue cooking until syrup forms a soft ball in cold water. Cool and beat until creamy. Add vanilla and baking powder and beat until thick. Spread on cake.

DRIED APPLES

Pare and slice your apples and spread on a cloth in the sunshine. Cover with fly netting, take them in at sunset and repeat daily until the apples pieces are brown and leathery. Hang in a paper bag in a dry place to keep.

BEAN PICKLE

Snap two pounds of fresh beans and wash them. Cover beans with three cups of boiling water and cook three minutes. Don't cover. Pack in preserving jars and pour over three cups of water mixed with a cup of vinegar, two tablespoons of salt and dill weed and two cloves of garlic. Can be kept for several weeks in a cool place.

BEET ROOT PICKLES

Drain the cooked beets, add to the juice three cups of sugar and a cup of vinegar, three teaspoonsful of ground cinnamon and a teaspoon of salt. Heat to boiling, add more vinegar if needed, pour over the beets and store a few days in a cool place before using. Shelled, hard-cooked eggs may be added.

COTTAGE CHEESE

Take a crock full of clabbered milk and set in on the hearth near the fire to heat just a little. When the whey and clabber separate, pour it in a jellybag and hang it up where it will drain 'til dry or put in a strainer lined with cheesecloth and place over a second bowl. Put in a little salt and some rich cream. Some like a little pepper. Mix with the hand and make into small balls to serve on a platter, or if much cream is used, serve in a dish.

DANDELION WINE

In a large crock pour two quarts of water over three pints of dandelion blossoms (pull off stems.) Let stand for six days. Strain through several thicknesses of cheesecloth. Add two pounds of sugar, one sliced lemon and two sliced oranges. Mix well and boil for a half an hour. Cool, pour into half gallon size bottles, and let stand for six months. Put into smaller bottles and seal.

MINCEMEAT FOR PIES

3 bowls beef
2 bowls cider
4 bowls sugar
5 bowls apples (including peel)
1 bowl suet
1 bowl molasses
1 bowl vinegar
½ bowl citron
2 bowls raisins
3 lemons (including rinds)
3 oranges (including rinds)
2 T. cinnamon
3 tsp. nutmeg
1 T. cloves
1 T. salt
1 T. pepper
1-2 bowls brandy or whiskey

Chop fine everything that needs to be chopped. Mix together in order. Store in a crock in a cool place. To use, place enough mincemeat to fill in pie plate lined with pastry. Top with second pastry, crimp edges and make several slits in top to release steam. Bake in moderate (375 degree) oven for 30 minutes or until golden brown.

SWEET PICKLES

4 quart medium cucumbers
1½ C. salt
4 quarts water
alum
9 cups vinegar
2 C. sugar
3 C. water
2 T. mixed pickle spices

Cut your cucumbers to one inch slices and put in a stone jar. Dissolve the salt in the 4 quarts of water and pour over the pickles. Add a chunk of alum the size of a two-bit piece. Cover and weight down and let stand a day and a half. Drain and wash pickles of alum. Put in a large kettle and pour over a quart of good vinegar and enough water to cover. Cook gently for 10 minutes. Pour off liquid. Mix two cups of sugar spices with 5 cups of vinegar and three cups of water. In cheesecloth bag tie up the spices and add to vinegar. Cook gently for 10 minutes. Pour over pickles in jar and let stand one full day. Remove spices and keep cool to eat.

Mrs. Zimmerman uses the small yellow bowl that holds about six cups to measure. If you don't want to make as much, just use a bowl about the size of a cup.

THE CAMPBELL HOUSE

Harriet Moore Campbell was born in 1798 on her father's tobacco plantation in Virginia. She married George Washington Campbell in 1818.

George had completed a three-year apprenticeship with a Lexington, Kentucky, doctor and received his certificate. In 1820, he inherited money from his father's estate and decided to use some of his inheritance to obtain his medical degree from Transylvania University. He decided that some of his money should be used for land speculation, and after learning of good land available in Indiana, he purchased 400 acres in Delaware Township, Hamilton County. He recorded his plat of Prairietown in 1831 and a year later moved his family members to their new home and began the practice of medicine.

During the winter of 1833, their only child, 2-year-old Horace William, suffered an attack of measles. Despite all of his medical knowledge the doctor was not able to save his son.

Mrs. Campbell, reared by an aristocratic family, is accustomed to household help. But Indiana is a free state, and slavery is outlawed. Mrs. Campbell was delighted when Dr. Campbell bought the contract of Maggie Miller, who was indigent. Maggie took over the cooking and cleaning chores. Abigail Bucher, daughter of a former neighbor, has been hired for household help and is learning to cook on the new-fangled stove.

Now, Mrs. Campbell has time to devote to raising the cultural status of the villagers.

CHICKEN AND OYSTERS

Fill your chickens with young oysters cut small, truffles, and parsley and roast them in a moderate (375 degree) oven until browned and juice runs clear when poked. Blanch about two dozen young oysters and toss them up in some melted butter, with chopped herbs and olive oil. When they have been on the fire a quarter of an hour, add a little white wine and half a glass (cup) of good stock, thicken it over the fire for another quarter of an hour, and when the chickens are ready to serve, pour the sauce on them, and garnish the dish with oysters and some lemon.

OYSTER PIE

Cook two chopped onions and one rib chopped celery in butter until golden and soft. In the same kettle, with the vegetables remaining, add three tablespoons of butter and the same of flour and mix well. Add one cup of milk and one-half cup of oyster liquor. Add dash of mace and thyme. Stir in one pint of oysters and cook until edges curl. Add sherry, enough to thin the sauce and stir. Add salt and mace if your tasting needs it, with pepper. Turn into baked pastry shell, put on top lid of pastry and bake in a moderate (375 degree) oven until pastry is done and pie is bubbly or 40-50 minutes. Minced parsley may be added to sauce.

SCALLOPED OYSTERS

Drain a quart of shucked oysters and warm over low heat in a kettle. Melt a half cup of butter and stir in two tablespoons of flour. Add to this two tablespoons each of minced green pepper and onion, a half clove of garlic that has been pressed, one tablespoon of lemon juice and one teaspoon spiced meat sauce (liquid store-bought sauce is acceptable) all mixed with a cup of fine cracker crumbs. Turn into a greased, shallow baking pan and put on a quarter cup of crumbs. Bake to a golden, light brown, in a moderate (375 degree) oven for about 30-40 minutes.

STUFFED EGGS

12 hard boiled eggs
3 large mushrooms
1 T. minced onion
butter
1 T. parsley, chopped
1 T. bread crumbs
1 T. lemon juice
1 T. prepared mustard
savory
salt and pepper to taste

Take a dozen shelled hard-boiled eggs, split them and mash up the yolks. Chop the mushrooms and saute them with the minced onion in butter in a skillet. Add the mushrooms to the yolks with everything else. Fill the whites of the eggs with it and lay them in a baking dish in which you have placed a layer of forcemeat made with chicken or veal. Bake them in a slow oven until they are brown and serve them hot with a mushroom sauce or a cream sauce seasoned with white wine.

TO DRESS DUCKS WITH JUICE OF ORANGES

The fresh ducks being singed, picked and drawn of feathers, mince the livers with a little scraped (sliced) bacon, some butter, green onions, sweet herbs and parsley, season with salt, and mushrooms. They being all minced together, put them into the bodies of the ducks, and roast the birds, covered with slices of bacon, and wrapped in cooking paper, in a moderate (375 degree) oven. In a separate pan, put a little gravy, the juice of an orange and a few onions minced, when the ducks are roasted enough (when they test tender with a fork and juices run clear), take off the bacon, dish them, and put your sauce with the juice of oranges over them, and serve them up hot.

TO ROAST A HAM OR GAMMON

Take off the swerd, or what we call the skin, or rind, and lay it in lukewarm water for two or three hours; then lay it in a pan, pour upon it a quart of canary,* and let it steep in it for 10 or 12 hours. When you have spitted it, put some sheets of white paper over the fat side, pour the canary in which it was soaked in the dripping-pan, and baste with it all the time it is roasting; when it is roasted enough (when it tests tender with a fork and juices run clear), pull off the paper, and dredge it well with crumbled bread and parsley shredded fine; make the fire brisk, and brown it well. If you eat it hot, garnish it with raspings of bread; if cold, serve it on a clean napkin, and garnish it with parsley for a second course.

*Canary—wine made in the Canary Islands, similar in character to Madeira.

FRENCH ROLLS

1 quart flour
½ tsp. salt
1 T. yeast
2 eggs
½ pint milk
1 ounce butter

Sift flour with salt, add yeast and the eggs, beaten. Put in milk. Knead it and set to rise. Next morning, work in an ounce of butter, make the dough into small rolls and bake them in a moderate (375 degree) oven for 30 minutes. The top crust should not be hard.

SALLY LUNN

½ C. warm water
1 large T. dry yeast
3 eggs, beaten
½ C. soft butter
¼ C. sugar
3 tsp. salt
1 C. warm milk
5½ C. flour

Put the water and yeast into a large bowl to dissolve. Add the beaten eggs, butter, sugar and salt with warm milk. Stir in three cups of flour and beat well. Stir in enough of the rest of the flour to make a soft dough. Cover and rise in a warm place until double, about an hour. Grease a Turk's Head mold or tube pan, dust with flour, stir down the dough and spoon into pan. Cover and let rise to double, another hour. Bake in fairly hot (400 degree) oven until a golden brown and a crust forms, about 30 minutes.

ASPARAGUS AND EGGS

Toast a slice of bread, butter it, and lay it on a dish; butter some eggs thus; take four eggs, beat them well, put them into a sauce pan with two ounces of butter (about 2 T.), and a little salt, cook until of a sufficient consistency, and put them on the toast; meanwhile boil some asparagus tender, cut the ends small, and lay them on the eggs.

YAMS WITH APPLES

Bake four large yams until tender. Meanwhile, pare four cooking apples and cut into thin slices. Peel yams, cut in slices about one-half inch thick. Arrange in layers with apples in a buttered baking pan. Sprinkle each layer with sugar and a dash of nutmeg. Dot with butter. Cover and bake half an hour in a moderate (350 degree) oven. Good with roast duck, game or ham.

BAKED SOUR APPLES

These are best baked in a stove. They require only an hour. There should be a little water in the tin. Bake in a moderate (350 degree) oven for about a half hour. When done, lay them in a dish, sprinkle a little brown sugar upon them, pour over what syrup remains in the tin, and cover them close till wanted for the table. They are good done in this way to eat at breakfast or tea, with bread and butter; and also at dinner, with any meat requiring apple sauce.

CHOCOLATE COOKIES

5 oz. dark chocolate
1 C. brown sugar
1 C. white sugar
1 C. lard
3 eggs
2 C. flour
1 tsp. soda
1 tsp. salt

1 T. vanilla
1 C. chopped nuts

Melt the chocolate and mix together with the sugars and lard. Add the eggs and beat well. Stir in all the rest and mix well. Put in a baking pan a teaspoon at a time, about three inches apart. Bake, until set, in a moderate (375 degree) oven for about 8 or 9 minutes.

FLOATING ISLAND

2 T. flour
4 C. milk
5 eggs
1/4 tsp. salt
3 T. sugar
1 tsp. vanilla or Rosewater

A good floating island is made by mixing the flour with 2 T. of milk from the 4 cups that are needed. In a large kettle, scald the rest of the milk. Beat 5 egg yolks in a small bowl. Add the flour and milk mixture to the yolks. Stir in half of the heated milk. Beat the egg whites very stiff and add the salt, sugar and flavoring. Drop egg mixture by spoonfuls into boiling water for two minutes. Float on the custard. Chill before serving.

ICING FOR CAKES

1 pound pulverized* sugar
3 egg whites
juice of 1 lemon
1 T. cornstarch

Beat the egg whites with the sugar and lemon juice. Add one teaspoonful of cornstarch and mix well. Flour the top of the cake as soon as taken from the oven and put on the icing with a large spoon, spreading by dipping a knife in cold water and smoothing over.

*confectioners

TEA CAKES

3/4 C. butter
1 tsp. vanilla
2 C. brown sugar
3 eggs
3 1/2 C. flour
1 tsp. soda
1/2 tsp. salt

Work the vanilla into the butter until soft, then add the brown sugar and cream well. Beat in three eggs, one at a time, and stir in flour, soda and the salt. Divide dough in half and chill several hours. Roll out as thin as possible on lightly floured board and cut in round shape. Bake in a moderate (350 degree) oven for about 9-10 minutes.

PLUM SAUCE

Wash one pound Damson plums, cut in half and remove pits. Combine fruit with one-half cup sugar in kettle. Add one stick cinnamon, one teaspoon whole mace and one teaspoon whole cloves tied together in a cheesecloth bag. Bring to boil, cook slowly over low fire until sauce has the same thickness as jam. Remove spices.

STRAWBERRY SUN JAM

Choose brightly colored berries that are not too ripe. It is difficult to prepare more than four or five quarts at a time. Wash, then drain very thoroughly. Removes hulls and slice berries in small pieces. Weigh the fruit, place in a large kettle and add sugar. For each pound of fruit allow three-fourths pound sugar. Stir until all berries are coated with sugar. Bring to a rolling boil and boil exactly three minutes. Pour immediately into flat dishes to a depth of one-half inch. The fruit should lie flat in the syrup. Cover completely with panes of glass and place outside in unobstructed sunlight. Turn glass covers each time enough moisture accumulates on top to pour off. Stir occasionally with a spoon to expose all surfaces of berries and syrup to the action of the sun. Strawberries are cooked when syrup forms jellied ridges or waves when container is tilted at one end. This usually takes about one and a half days of full sunshine. Bottle immediately. If rainy or cloudy weather should interfere, bring dishes, tightly covered, inside. Strawberries will keep safely for several days if fruit has cooked for four or five hours.

BON-BONS

Cook 1 C. sugar, 2 C. brown sugar and ½ C. rich milk until it reaches the soft ball stage. Pour into a buttered bowl and when cool beat in a teaspoon of vanilla and a tablespoon of butter until creamy. Knead until firm and form into ropes about an inch in diameter. Chop into bonbon size. Decorate the pieces with citron, nuts or shaved chocolate. Dip some into hot melted chocolate before decorating.

CANDIED FLOWERS AND LEAVES

Use borage flowers, violets or rose petals when in full bloom: leaves of catnip, horehound, lemon balm, mint or sage, which are tender and unspotted. Rinse with water, dry. Dip flowers or leaves into a well beaten mixture of whites of two eggs, one tablespoon each of lemon juice and water. When thoroughly coated, sprinkle them with fine granulated sugar until completely covered. Spread on greased paper to dry.

CANDIED PEEL

Cut the rind of eight oranges into quarters and cover with cold water in a kettle or pan. Boil slowly for about 12 minutes. Take from the fire, drain and repeat four more times. Drain the peel and cut into strips. Make a syrup of one cup of water and two of sugar. Put peel into the syrup and boil until all syrup is absorbed. Cool.

Roll in sugar, dry on paper. Store in a loose container.

HOT SPICED PUNCH

Simmer a quart of apple cider with three cinnamon sticks, four tablespoonsful of lemon juice and let it simmer about quarter of an hour. Tie a well broken whole nutmeg and a teaspoonful of whole cloves in a small cheesecloth bag and put into the simmering cider long enough to satisfy your taste.

STRAWBERRY WINE

Mash one gallon of good berries and add a half gallon of boiling water. Let stand twenty-four hours. Strain and add three pounds of brown sugar to each gallon of juice. Let stand thirty-six hours, skimming off scum. Put in a cask, saving some to add as it escapes. Fill each morning with more water. Cork and seal when done working.

WASSAIL BOWL

In a five-quart brass or copper kettle, empty a gallon of apple cider and put to it two cups of juice from Seville oranges, juice and the rinds of two lemons and two cups of sugar. Add your spices: two teaspoons of ground allspice, five sticks of cinnamon, bring to a boil and simmer slowly for fifteen minutes. Add three cups of apple brandy and serve piping hot to forty people. A nice addition is to float boiled apples in your wassail. Core six red apples and place in a saucepan with a cup of water. Pour over the apples a half cup of sugar and boil gently until apples are tender. Turn the apples a few times while they cook. Drain and float the apples in your punch bowl filled with wassail. Save the syrup. It will be nice on your next pudding.

KITCHEN PEPPER

Mix to the finest powder, one ounce of ginger. Add cinnamon, black pepper, nutmeg and Jamaica pepper, half an ounce each. Also, ten cloves and six ounces of salt. Keep it in a bottle—it is an agreeable addition to any brown sauces or to soups.

BOURBON PECAN CAKE

- 2 tsp. nutmeg
- 1/2 C. bourbon
- 1 1/2 C. sifted all-purpose flour, divided
- 2 C. pecans
- 1 C. raisins, finely chopped
- 1/2 C. butter
- 1 C. plus 2 T. sugar
- 3 eggs, separated
- 1 tsp. baking powder
- dash salt
- pecan halves

Preheat oven to 325°. Grease a 10″ tube pan. Soak nutmeg in bourbon.

Mix 1/2 C. flour with the nuts and raisins, coating thoroughly. Reserve.

Cream butter and sugar until light and fluffy. Add egg yolks, one at a time, beating well after each addition. Beat in remaining flour, baking powder and salt. Beat in bourbon-nutmeg mixture and continue beating until batter is well mixed. Add the nuts and raisins. Beat the egg whites until very stiff. Fold in. Spoon batter into pan. Press down firmly to squeeze out air pockets and allow to stand 10 minutes. Bake at 325° for 1 1/4 hours or until cake tests done.

Cool in the pan, right side up, 1 to 2 hours before turning out. Continue cooling.

This cake improves with age. Store in a covered container for several days, wrapped in a bourbon-soaked napkin.

Custard pies are finished baking when a knife blade inserted in the middle comes out clean. Fruit pies are finished when they bubble nicely.

A CABINET OF CURIOSITIES 1830 - 1850

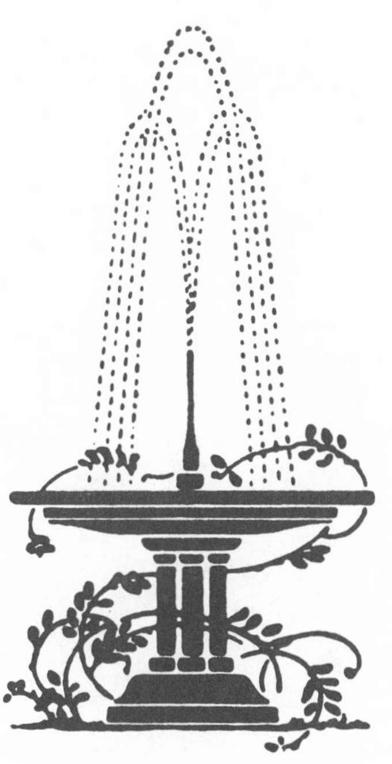

W. C. COUP MANAGER of
PROF. WORTH'S MUSEUM OF A MILLION FEATURES,
AND
LEVANTINE'S AGGREGATION OF NOVELTIES!
INTRODUCING A SELECTION OF
OPERATIC and SPECIALTY STARS
IN GRAND STAGE PERFORMANCES.

AN ASTOUNDING CONJUNCTION OF STARTLING SENSATIONS AND CLASSICALLY-BEAUTIFUL PERFORMANCES.

Circuses and grand menageries travelled through Indiana from 1830 on, displaying clowns, wonders and bareback riders as well as exotic animals.

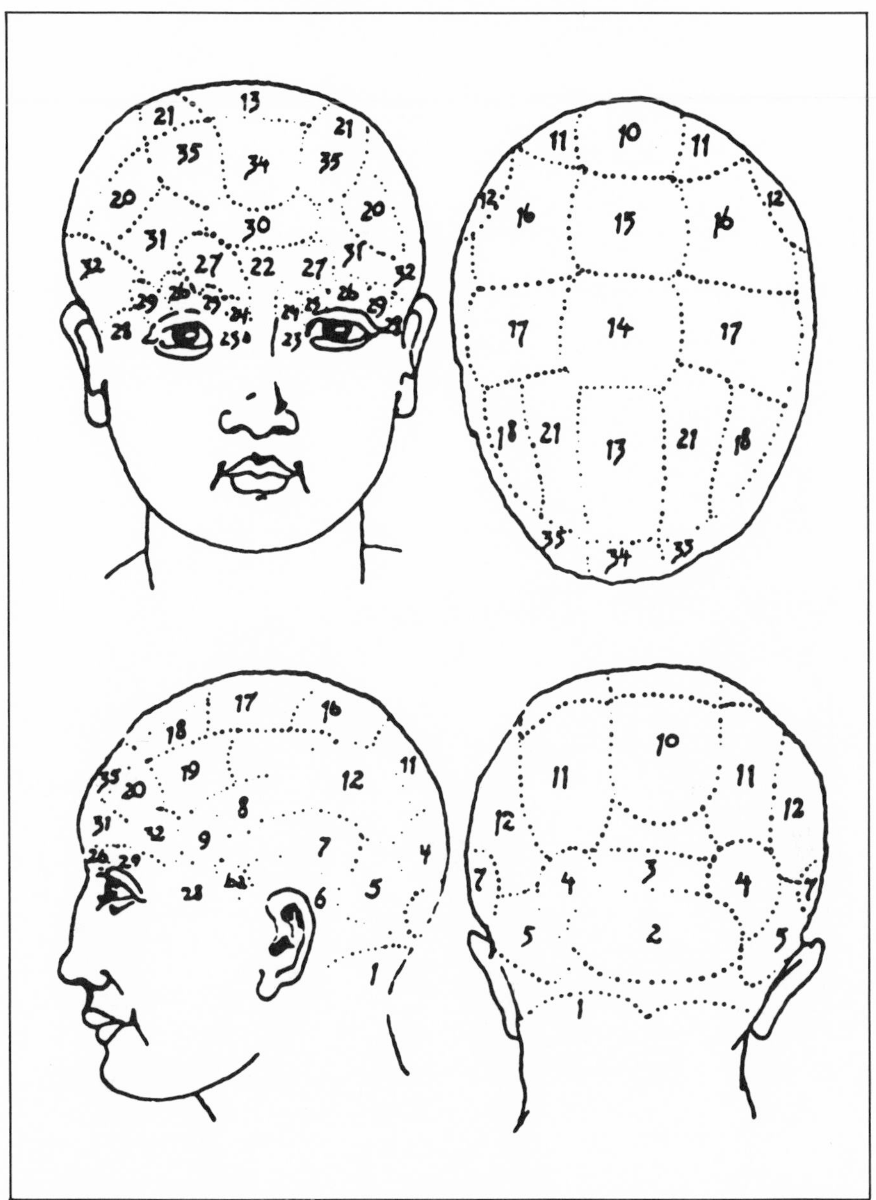

Phrenology was a passion with many people. Travelling practitioners spoke on raised platforms in the center of Indiana villages about the new "science" by which they could determine a person's characteristics by the shape of his or her head.

Unidentified Artist, *"A Narrow Escape from a Snake,"* woodcut. From *Davy Crockett's Almanack*, 1838.

Snakes were a real danger in Indiana, but this cartoon reptile makes fun of frontier tall tales.

In the 1830s George Winter painted a picture of a trap people set to capture an alleged "lake monster" which supposedly lurked in Lake Manitou in Northern Indiana.

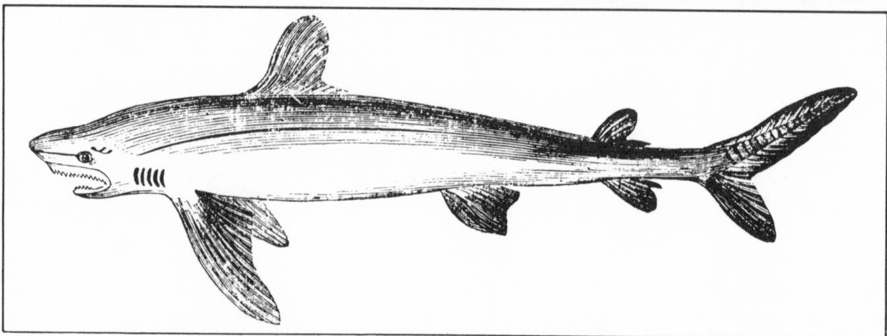

Natural history was a fascination. Here are goats and sharks from a magazine of the times.

Fitness is nothing new. Godey's Ladies Book *shows how young belles may use dumbells and rods to strengthen their arms in the 1850s when women had more leisure.*

A Prairie.

A Prairie on Fire.

Shakers believed God entered the faithful when they danced. Non-believers often attended shaker meetings to marvel.

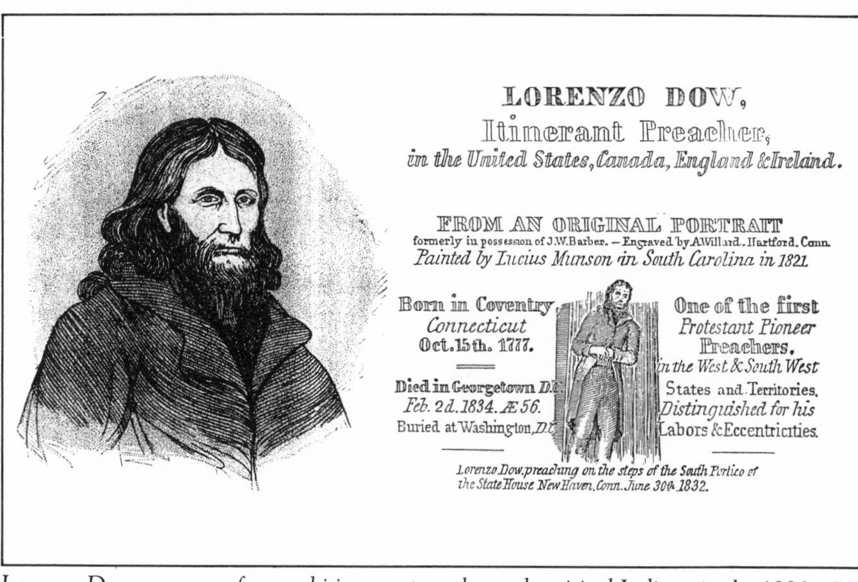

Lorenzo Dow was one of several itinerant preachers who visited Indiana in the 1830s. He often got "took by the Lord" and ended up crawling around on all fours on the ground.

The late 1830s saw the forced expulsion of Indiana's Potawatomi and slightly later, the Miami. This Potawatomi band chief was painted by artist George Winter.

The popular Royal couple of England, Victoria and Albert were often discussed in newspapers, even in rural Indiana.

THE FENTON HOUSE

Grace and Alexander Fenton, a weaver, came from Chester County, South Carolina and settled on a farm on the outskirts of Hamilton County. Not really a farmer at heart, Alex purchased land from Dr. Campbell in 1834, built a house and left their only son, Robert, and his wife, Sarah Mary, to tend the farm. He moved Mrs. Fenton to the village, built himself a loom and proceeded to practice his weaving trade. Alex works with wool, cotton and linen and some of his finished products are traded to Mr. Whitaker for provisions that Mrs. Fenton needs to keep body and soul together.

In addition to their vegetable garden, the Fentons grow various herbs. Some of the plants are used to obtain dye to give pleasing color to the wool that Mr. Fenton weaves into cloth. As important to the Fentons, who are believers of Thomsonian medicine, are the herbs that are needed for their medicinal concoctions. This belief is the source of disgust to neighbor Dr. Campbell and results in behind-the-back snickering by many neighbors. A wonder to the rest of the townspeople is their practice of "leaking of the skin"* to relieve common ailments.

*"leaking of the skin" means sweating

GREEN CORN SOUP

2 C. fresh young ears of corn
2 C. water
1 tsp. salt
pepper to taste
2 T. butter
2 T. flour
2 C. milk
1 onion

Grate and scrape the corn from the cobs and boil it in two cups of water five minutes. Add salt and pepper and then melt the butter, blend in the flour, put in with the corn. Cook about three minutes. Mix with the milk and turn into into the kettle with the corn. Drop in the onion and cook slowly for ten minutes. Take out the onion and serve the soup up hot.

POTATO AND ONION SOUP

2 onions
3 potatoes
lump of butter
½ pint milk
salt and pepper
1 C. cream

Take two onions, slice thin, fry in a pan until golden brown in the lump of butter. Clean and cut three pared potatoes very small—lay them on top of the onions until they, too, are brown. Pour over them one-half pint of milk with the salt and pepper. Cook slow until tender. Remove from fire then stir in a cup of good cream.

BAKED HEART

1 beef heart
1 C. vinegar
1 receipt of forcemeat

Soak the heart for an hour in cold water to which one cup of vinegar has been added. Remove the heart and cut off any fat. Boil for one hour. Remove and stuff with forcemeat, then tie together. Put in a kettle with a little water and cook for two or three hours until tender. Make sure the kettle does not boil dry.

ROASTED SMALL GAME BIRDS

4 small game birds
2 slices dry bread
4 T. butter
¼ C. pecans
Sherry wine

Clean your birds and set aside. Crumble the dry bread and cook in half the butter for a minute or two. Mix the chopped pecans and add to bread with enough sherry to moisten. Stuff the birds until plump and close the cavities with small skewers. Truss legs and wings close to bodies with string and place in a shallow baking pan. Add just enough water to cover the bottom of the pan. Brush the birds with the rest of the butter, melted, and bake 30 minutes in a moderate to quick (375 degree) oven, basting often with melted butter. Birds will be done when golden brown and juices run clear when poked.

SPICED NEATS TONGUE

Take a tongue, let it stew in water just to cover for two hours, then peel it, put it back in the water with half a pint of white wine, a bundle of sweet herbs (basil, marjoram, thyme and rosemary), a little salt and pepper, some mace and cloves tied in a muslin bag, a spoonful of capers chopped, turnips and carrots sliced, a piece of butter rolled in flour; let all stew together very softly over a slow fire for two hours, then take out the spices and sweet herbs, and send it to the table. You may leave out the turnips and carrots, or boil them by themselves, and lay them in a dish, just as you like.

TO BOIL FOWLS

Dust the fowls with flour, put them in a kettle of cold water, cover it close, set it on the fire; when the scum begins to rise, take it off, let them boil very slowly for twenty minutes, then take them off, cover them close, and the heat of the water will stew them in half an hour; it keeps the skin whole, and they will be both whiter and plumper than if they had boiled fast; when you take them up, drain them and pour over them white sauce or melted butter.

TO MAKE AN OMELETTE

Break six or eight eggs in a dish, beat a little, add parsley and chives chopped small, with pepper and salt, mix all well together, put a piece of butter in a spider or pan, let it melt over a clear fire until nearly brown, pour in the eggs, stir it in, and in a few minutes it will be sufficiently done, double or fold it and dish it quite hot.

TO MAKE WHITE SAUCE FOR FOWLS

Take a scrag of veal, the necks of fowls, or any bits of mutton or veal you have, put them in a sauce pan with a blade or two of mace, a few black pepper corns, a head of celery, a bunch of sweet herbs, a slice of the end of a lemon; put in a quart of water and cover it close, let it boil till it is reduced to half a pint, strain it, and thicken with a quarter of a pound of butter mixed with flour, boil it five or six minutes, put in two spoonsful of pickled mushrooms. Mix the yolks of two eggs with a teacup of good cream and a little nutmeg—put it in the sauce, keep shaking it over the fire, but don't let it boil.

BISCUITS

Mix a pound of flour, the yolk of an egg, and some milk into a very stiff paste; beat it well, knead till quite smooth, roll very thin and cut into biscuits, prick and bake in a slow (300 degree) oven till dry and crisp, or for about 20 minutes.

CRACKERS

Put together one egg white, one tablespoon butter, one teacup sweet milk, one-half teaspoon of soda and a teaspoon cream of tartar. Add flour to make very stiff, roll thin and bake until golden and set.

TO COOK DRIED CORN

Place one cup dried corn in kettle, pour on two cups of boiling water, let stand at least one hour. Then stir in two teaspoons sugar, one-half teaspoon salt and two tablespoons butter. Cook, uncovered, over a low heat for half an hour. Stir in one-half cup cream and cook five minutes longer.

HERB TO MAKE TEA

The following may be combined to make tea:

Sage, rosemary and thyme
Lemon verbena and mint
Rose hips and mint
comfrey and mint
Thyme and hyssop
Catnip, mint, sage and chamomile
Mint with either sage or lemon balm

Sweeten with honey.

THE BAKER HOUSE

Lucinda Baker, wife of potter Isaac Baker, spent all of her single years in the woods and knows every type of tree, wild herb, wild flower and every breed of animal and its habitat. Never formally educated, she does not know how to read and can only write her name.

Since her marriage and move to the village she has slowly become accustomed to close neighbors and even finds enjoyment in visiting with a few new-found friends.

Not given to much domesticity, Lucinda would rather throw a groundhog into the pot to cook for Isaac and his two unmarried brothers, Levi and Jonathan, and spend her time fishing, hunting in the woods, weaving a basket or wedging clay in the pottery for her husband. Occasionally Lucinda's mother, Kate Bend, will pay a visit and might take over the cooking chores, but she also was raised in the backwoods and isn't any more "persnickety" than her daughter when it comes to keeping things clean and tidy.

Mrs. Curtis, Lucinda's friend, wrote all but the first of the Baker section of the collection of Prairietown receipts. Although Lucinda doesn't read or write there may be a member in the future generations of her family who will be fortunate enough to have some sort of an education. Mary Curtis is convinced that old family receipts are to be treasured.

TO COOK A RABBIT

"A good cleer firr will rost a yung rabbit in bout an hour. Put flour to it, fry in buter. Maak it a fine brown. Take out the rabbit and chop its livar, biled, put it in tha graby."

TO MAKE PEAS-PORRIDGE

Take a quart of green peas, put them to a quart of boiling water, a bundle of dried mint, and a little salt. Let them boil till the peas are quite tender; then put in some beaten pepper, a piece of butter as big as a walnut, rolled in flour, stir all together, and let it boil a few minutes, then add two quarts of milk, let it cook a quarter of an hour, take out the mint, and serve it up.

DODGERS

Mix together a cup of cornmeal with one teaspoon salt and one and a half teaspoons of sugar. Pour over one cup of boiling water. Add a tablespoon of butter or bacon drippings. Shape into cakes with your hands, place on greased griddle and fry until golden brown.

FRIED BISCUITS

Mix one and three quarter cups of bread flour with one teaspoon salt, three teaspoons baking powder, one teaspoon sugar, a half teaspoon baking soda, four tablespoons butter or lard and two-thirds to three-quarters cup buttermilk or sour milk. Turn onto floured board and knead quickly for half a minute. Pat to a quarter inch thickness, cut in shapes. Fry in hot lard until browned on each side. Good with butter and molasses.

JOHNNY CAKES

In bowl, beat two eggs and mix in one cup of water, two tablespoons of lard, melted, one teaspoon salt and three-quarters cup milk. Stir in two cups of cornmeal. Cook on greased griddle until golden. Put to table with butter and maple syrup.

FRIED VENISON

Take venison steaks, about one inch thick, cut into small pieces and brown on all sides in a spider with melted butter. Turn often to prevent burning. Add more butter if necessary, with salt and pepper to season. Cook until slightly pink.

SALT FISH

Salt fish should be put in a deep plate, with just enough water to cover it, the night before you intend to cook it. It should not be boiled an instant;

boiling renders it hard. It should lie in scalding water two or three hours. The less water is used, the more fish is cooked at once, the better. Water thickened with flour while boiling, with sweet better put in to melt is the common sauce.

Salted Mackerel should be put into a deep plate and covered with boiling water for about ten minutes before it is thoroughly broiled, before it is buttered. This makes it tender, takes off the coat of salt, and prevents the strong oily taste, so apt to be unpleasant in preserved fish.

Salt fish mashed with potatoes, with good butter or pork scraps to moisten it, is nicer the second day than it was the first. The fish should be minced very fine, while it is warm. After it has got cold and dry, it is difficult to do nicely. Salt fish needs plenty of vegetables, such as onions, beets, carrots, &c.

There is no way of preparing salt fish for breakfast so nice as to roll it up in little balls, after it is mixed with mashed potatoes; dip it in an egg, and fry it brown.

TO DRESS DUCKS WITH ONIONS

Singe, pick and draw the ducks, cut the roots off small onions, blanch them in scalding water, then pick and put them into a stew pan with a little gravy, set them over a gentle fire, and let them simmer, when they are done, thicken them with cream and flour and when the ducks are roasted, dish them, pour the ragout of onions over, and serve up hot. The ducks may be stuffed with a nice forcemeat.

TO FRY PERCH

Clean the fish nicely, but do not take out the roes, dry them on a cloth, sprinkle some salt, and dredge them with flour, lay them separately on a board, when one side is dry, turn them, sprinkle salt and dredge the other side, be sure the lard boils when you put the fish in, and fry them with great care, they should be a yellowish brown when done. Send melted butter or anchovy sauce in a boat.

HASTY PUDDING

Bring to boil six cups of water, add one teaspoon of salt and slowly pour in one cup of cornmeal. Stir until the mixture is thick and smooth. Set over hot water and steam for about one half hour.

A FLOUR PUDDING

One quart of milk scalded, add five spoons flour to milk while hot; when cool add seven eggs well beaten, six ounces sugar, salt, cinnamon, nutmeg to your taste, bake one hour, serve up with sweet sauce.

PEACH LEATHER

To six pounds of ripe peaches, pared and quartered, allow three pounds of the best brown sugar. Mix them together and put them in a preserving kettle, with barely enough water to keep them from burning, then pound and mash them with a wooden beetle. Then boil and skim them for three hours, stirring them nearly all the time. When done, spread them thinly on large dishes and set them in the sun to dry for three or four days. (Bring them in at night.) Finish the drying by loosening the leather from the dishes and setting them in the oven after the bread is taken out, letting them remain until the oven is cold. Roll up the leather and put it away in a box. Apple leather may be made in the same manner.

TO DRY CORN

To each eight pints of raw corn, cut off, add six tablespoons of sugar, four teaspoons coarse salt and one-half cup of sweet cream. Boil for twenty minutes in kettle while stirring all the time so the mixture does not stick. Then, spread the cooked corn in a shallow pan, or pans, and stir the grain often as it dries. When the kernels are crisp dump them into clean bags made of brown paper. Tie securely and hang in driest room. It will be completely dry when it rattles in the sacks. It is delicious when cooked in cream and butter.

THE CURTIS HOUSE

When the Curtis family arrived in Indiana from Canandiagua in the state of New York in 1834, they were pleased to find such a good farm, nice house and well-stocked blacksmith shop. Ben had purchased the property from Lucas Wainscott, sight unseen, after reading an advertisement in a trade journal.

After the long trip, by steamboat and by freight wagon, it was a relief to the family to settle down and get to know their neighbors. Ruth Curtis, Ben's older sister, traveled to Indiana with them and is a source of help and comfort to Mary Curtis and their three children, Thomas, age 7, Jenny, age 5, and Edward, who is 3 years.

Ben does good work and hopes someday to make as much money as the doctor. Then he'll make his house modern for Mary . . . maybe even buy her a cookstove. Until then, she has worked to make their house nice, stenciling the parlor floors and walls.

Mary enjoys visiting with the other ladies in the village, especially when there's a "quilting frolic" and they get a chance to exchange receipts.

CHOWDER

Fry a third-cup of diced salt pork in a heavy kettle and add a sliced onion and cook until soft but not browned. Add three cups of diced potatoes and three cups of boiling water. Cover and cook slow until the potatoes are done. Put in two and a half cups of corn, cut from the cob, four cups of milk and some salt and pepper. Should not boil. Stir in six large hard crackers before serving up.

OXTAIL SOUP

Cut oxtail into pieces and put in a large kettle with two whole cloves, one teaspoon of salt, one-quarter teaspoon pepper and one quart of water. Cook until meat is tender. Then cool. Strain and remove all the fat but keep the meat and broth. Brown one sliced onion and the oxtail meat in butter. Return to the broth with one sliced carrot, one chopped turnip and half a cup of chopped celery. Cook until vegetables are tender and stir in one teaspoon of lemon juice and serve.

TO COOK A GOOD BEAN SOUP

Give your dried beans (about two pounds) a good washing and put them in a kettle with plenty of water and a good, meaty ham bone. If to your taste, add a chopped onion. Cook until the beans are tender, adding salt and pepper to taste. Add water when needed to keep from burning. This should take 3 to 4 hours.

GOOSE

A good goose should be stuffed with sage and onion, chopped small, and mixed with pepper and salt; boil the sage and onions in a little water before they are chopped, or mix a few bread crumbs with them when chopped; either will render them less strong. Put it first at a distance from the fire, and by degree draw it nearer. A slip of paper should be skewered on the breast bone. Baste it very well. When the breast is risen, take off the paper, and be careful to serve it before the breast falls, it will be spoiled by coming to the table flattened.

MEAT CAKES

Take whatever meat, game or poultry you may chance to have (it is better for being under-done). Mince it fine, adding a little fat bacon or ham, season with a little pepper and salt; mix the whole together well, and make it into small cakes, about three inches in length, an inch and a half in width and half an inch thick. Fry them to a light brown and serve them with a good gravy, or put it into a mould, and bake it.

A reasonable indulgence in the abundant supplies of nature, converted by art to the purposes of wholesome food, is one of the comforts added to the maintenance of life."
—The Cook's Own Book, *by a Boston Housekeeper (Mrs. N.K.M. Lee), 1832*

TO ROAST VENISON

Remove all bone and fat, tie if necessary, and brown in fat in a deep spider or dutch oven, after roast has been dusted with flour. Cook slowly adding a small amount of water from time to time if the pot begins to cook dry. When about half done, add four large carrots that have been sliced, several onions cut small. This is the time to add salt, pepper and any sweet herbs that you favor. Baste frequently as you would a turkey. Done when tested with fork and juices run clear (about 20 minutes per pound).

BATTER BREAD

2 C. flour
1/2 tsp. salt
1/2 tsp. soda
1/2 tsp. baking powder
2 T. sugar
2 T. butter
1 egg
3/4 C. sour milk

Mix flour, salt, soda, baking powder, sugar and butter. Put in the egg and sour milk and mix well. Turn out onto bread board and knead it a little, then put it in a spider and bake to a nice golden brown in a moderate oven (350 degrees) for 25-30 minutes. Or, pat out in a large circle, spread with butter and brown sugar and fold over to make a nice sweet bread.

CREAM OF TARTAR BISCUITS

2 C. flour
2 tsp. cream of tartar
1 tsp. soda
1 tsp. salt
1/4 C. butter
1 C. light cream

Sift the flour through a hair sieve* and put in cream of tartar, soda and salt. Cut in the butter and moisten with cream. Knead with as few stokes as possible, working rapidly. Pat out to half an inch thick and cut into biscuit shapes. Bake in a moderate (350 degree) oven until golden brown, about 20 minutes.

*Or, use a sifter or strainer.

FRITTERS

Put a piece of butter the size of an egg into a pint of water, let it boil up a few minutes. Thicken it very smoothly with a pint of flour. Let it remain a short time on the fire, stirring it all the time so that it may not stick to the pan. Pour it in a wooden bowl, add five or six eggs, breaking one and beating it in, then another, and so on 'til they are all in and the dough is quite light. Put a pint of lard in a pan and let it boil. Make the fritters small, and fry them of a fine amber color.

GRAHAM CRACKERS

To one quart of graham flour put in one and one-third cups of very cold water and knead very hard for fully twenty minutes, using more flour if the dough is not stiff enough. Roll out like pie-crust, cut in shapes, prick with a fork, and bake fifteen minutes in a moderate over. Let get cold before putting away.

NOODLES

1 C. flour
3 whole eggs
salt
butter the size of a walnut
½ egg shell of cold water

Mix well and turn onto a bread board, knead in the flour to make a stiff dough. Roll into sheets, let dry and cut into very thin strips. Let dry again. Store in a cool, dry place until needed.

PANCAKES—COMMON

½ pound flour
5 eggs
1 quart milk

With nearly half a pound of flour, mix five well-beaten eggs, and then add, by degrees, a quart of good milk and a little salt. Fry them in fresh lard, and serve them with pounded loaf-sugar strewed between each.

BAKED SQUASH

2 squash
4 slices bacon
salt and pepper
brown sugar

Wash the squash and cut them in half. Spoon out the seeds and fibers from the cavity. Put the bacon in a shallow baking pan and bake until crisp. Remove from heat and drain and save fat. Sprinkle the squash with salt and pepper and place, cut side down, in bacon fat. Bake until tender in a moderate (375 degree) oven. Before serving, sprinkle with brown sugar and dribble on bacon fat, then drop the bacon, crumbled, into cavities. Winter, acorn or any squash will do just fine.

CARROT FRITTERS

2-3 boiled carrots
6 eggs
1 C. flour
2-3 T. sugar
cream or white wine

Beat the carrots to a pulp with a spoon then add the eggs and flour. Moisten them with cream or white wine and sweeten them with sugar. Beat all together well and fry in boiling lard. When of a good color, take them from the lard and squeeze on them the juice of a Seville orange, and strew over fine sugar.

BREAD PUDDING

4 C. stale bread
3 C. warm milk
salt
3 eggs
1 tsp. vanilla
½ tsp. nutmeg
½ C. sugar

Crumble the stale bread and soak for 20 minutes in the warm milk to which has been added a little salt. Mix the eggs, vanilla, nutmeg and sugar in and beat well. Pour in a pudding pan set in a spider or pan. Put an inch of water in the spider so the pudding will steam. Bake until set in a moderate (375 degree) oven for about 25 minutes. Good served with a sauce or fruit.

CHRISTMAS COOKIES

- 1 pound brown sugar
- 1 quart molasses
- ½ pound butter
- ½ pound lard
- 2 T. cinnamon
- 1 T. ginger
- 1 T. cloves
- 1 T. soda
- 6 C. flour

Put the brown sugar to the molasses and mix well. Melt the butter and lard together, cool and add to brown sugar mixture. Put in cinnamon, ginger, cloves, soda and three cups of the flour. Mix well. Add the rest of the flour, mix again. Let stand overnight. Roll very thin on a floured breadboard and cut into shapes. Bake on greased tins in a moderate (375 degree) oven for about 8 minutes. Makes about six pounds.

PUMPKIN PIE

- 3 C. pumpkin pulp
- 4-5 eggs
- 1½ C. sugar
- 1 tsp. salt
- 1 tsp. cinnamon
- 1 tsp. ginger
- ½ tsp. cloves
- 2½ C. rich milk
- 1 receipt of pie pastry

Pare your pumpkin or squash, take out the seeds and stew it until cooked. Strain it and run it through a colander. Mix the pulp with the eggs, sugar, salt and spices. Stir in the milk. Put your pastry into two pie dishes and make a nice edge on each, pour in your filling and bake in a moderate (350 degree) oven until done, about 40 minutes. A knife inserted into the middle of the pie will come out clean when done.

SUGAR COOKIES

1 C. butter
2 C. sugar
3 eggs
½ tsp. grated lemon peel
1 tsp. nutmeg
1 tsp. salt
¾ tsp. cream of tartar
4½ C. flour

Work the butter into the sugar. Of the three eggs, save one white and beat up the remaining eggs and add to butter. Add the rest and mix well. Roll to one-half inch thick and cut into shapes. Bake in a quick (400 degree) oven for 8-10 minutes.

LEMONADE

Roll six lemons well, cut in half and squeeze out the juice. Strain and add sugar to your liking. Pour one cup boiling water over the lemon rinds and let stand until cold. Strain and add to juice with eight cups very cold water. The hot water extracts the oil from the rinds and thus adds greatly to the flavor. Add a little ice to each mug. Very refreshing for the sick and aged.

APPLEBUTTER

Pare, core and slice your apples and cook with a little water until a good sauce (or until soft). To four cups of the sauce put in two cups of sugar, brown or white, two cups of apple cider, a half-teaspoon each of ground cloves and nutmeg and a sprinkle of allspice. Some add a spoonful of cinnamon. Cook without covering in a brass or copper kettle. Do not let burn. Let it be a good dark brown color and translucent. If your cider is hard or turned to vinegar it will still make a good butter.

MOLASSES CANDY

Dissolve a cup of sugar in half a cup of vinegar and then mix with a quart of molasses and boil, stirring constantly until a drop from the spoon into cold water hardens. Remove from heat and stir in butter the size of a egg and one teaspoon of soda. Pour into buttered pans. Cut into pieces as the candy begins to cool.

RECIPES FOR SPECIAL OCCASIONS AND GENERAL INFORMATION

VIANDS FOR AN AFTERNOON TEA

Young Hyson Tea
Pineapple Cheese
Smoked Tongue
Crackers
Tea Cakes with Icing
Maids of Honor
Filberts
Almonds
Brazil Nuts

Do not brew your tea until time to use it. Keeping it over the fire to keep hot for a long period of time tends to make it bitter and untasteful. It is best kept in a stoneware or china pot. Offer light cream, devoid of butter fat, and fine white sugar to enhance your tea.

Slice your cheese and smoked tongue in very thin slices and arrange on a china plate, with the crackers in a basket. Foods for afternoon tea are never intended to replace an evening meal so should be light and not too filling. Your tea party should not begin until late afternoon and three hours should be long enough.

If unavailable from Mr. Whitaker's store you can purchase your needs from McCarty and Nicholas, Indianapolis grocery merchants. They have in stock most of the articles needed for this tea party. Advertised in the Indiana Journal, August, 1836.

FANCY FOODS FOR A FESTAL BOARD

Barbecued Pig with Plum Sauce
Roasted Potatoes
Scalloped Oysters
Dried Corn
Mincemeat Pie
Carrot Fritters
Wheat Bread
Rye Bread
Biscuits
Pickles
Brandied Peaches
Bean Pickle
Chocolate Cookies
White Cookies
Petticoat Tails
Pine Tree Shillings
Applesauce Cake
Bon-Bons
Candied Peel
Wassail Bowl of Hot Spiced Punch with Boiled Apples

It is never prudent to concern yourself with the state of another person's taste. There is seldom found, on this frontier, a citizen who will decline anything offered if it is food and especially if the person is a weary traveler. I have known of travelers who went for many days with no sustenance other than an unwary rabbit and a handful of berries. How they must have longed for the sight of a table such as this. It is food for the soul when a host can offer a feast to his fellow mortals.

EATABLES FOR A PICNIC

Meat Cakes
Ham and Pork Loaf
Head Cheese
Cream of Tartar Biscuits
Corn Bread
Butter and Jam
Pickles
Beet Root Pickled with Hard Cooked Eggs
Gingerbread
Lemonade
Doughnuts

A picnic is a festive occasion whether it be a celebration or simply to deliver repast to the busy laborer. To leave a task that is unfinished to partake of a noon meal, if there are several miles to travel, is not necessary if the female neighbors gather together and prepare food for a picnic and transport it to the site of the labor. Time is dear and daylight hours can be short. Ladies, let your labours be labours of love and delight in the gratitude expressed for both your consideration and your talents for dressing the table.

FOOD FOR SPRINGTIME SPLENDOR

Preparing a company dinner is a simple matter during the summer and fall growing season but not so simple during the winter when snow and ice cover the ground. Oh, the glory of spring when the tender tips of salat greens begin poking through the earth, just waiting to be savored. Woe unto those who neglected to store enough vinegar from the apples of last fall. Nothing will herald the arrival of a new growing season any more than will a big bowl of salat sprinkled with sweetened vinegar. Resist the urge to fry up a heaping platter of chicken. The spring chickens will not be big enough to bother with until Independence Day. If your cider has thawed since the weather has begun to warm up you must serve it sparingly. It is probably quite hard or may have turned to vinegar.

USE AND CARE OF COOKING EQUIPMENT

The number of people who are seriously collecting antique kitchen equipment seems to be growing and the availability is decreasing. Antique parlor furniture, primarily used for company and certainly, never subjected to the rough and tumble use of children, is still relatively easy to find. The family pewter tableware, used several times daily by a family because of necessity, is rapidly disappearing. Pewter at one time was highly regarded but when more and more people were able to afford coin silver their pewter knives, forks, plates, bowls and chargers were relegated to, and subjected to, the rigors of the kitchen. Many of the treasures of yesterday are being fairly accurately reproduced today. Whether you are using antiques or reproductions the care is pretty much the same. Here are just a few tips to help you care for or restore your equipment.

1. Never leave water standing for any long period in iron pots, kettles or skillets.

2. Do not place any empty pot or kettle in or over the fire unless for the purpose of quick drying.

3. After using wash iron cooking utensils, including lids, with hot, soapy water, rinse well and dry thoroughly. Place them near or over the fire for quick drying and remove as soon as dry. If using a modern stove, dry in the oven at 150-200 degrees for 15-20 minutes.

4. NEVER store iron pots with the lid in place. They will acquire a musty odor and accumulate moisture. Rust will result.

5. It is better to boil out burned on food. Never try to soak out whether it be iron, copper or brass.

6. Wooden utensils should be washed thoroughly after each use. Do not allow to soak. The same applies to wooden or burl bowls. After washing, dry well and oil lightly.

7. Wooden buckets, if used, should be kept full of water and not allowed to completely dry. Drying out will cause the wood to shrink and they will not hold water. They should be scrubbed out every other day and refilled.

8. If your mantle is equipped with a utensil rack it is best, when cooking, to refrain from hanging the utensils you are using until you are through

cooking. Then wash them and replace on the rack. "Out of sight, out of mind." If you hang what you're using you'll forget to clean it.

9. Never, ever, use pewter or silver for cooking. Wash and dry after every use. Wash with a mild detergent. Pewter will melt at a lower temperature than silver but it is never advisable to use either as a cooking utensil. Each time a pewter spoon is used to stir or scrape it loses a little of the metal. Just a pewter spoon handle isn't good for much of anything.

10. If you own a copper or brass tea kettle and want to use it be sure you also own a trivet. Put your kettle on the hearth on the trivet a fair distance from the fire. If you hang the kettle on the crane over the fire you may not have a tea kettle long. Most of them are welded and the weld will melt in high heat.

11. As a general rule, only cook fruits and milk products in copper or brass. Acid foods will help maintain the copper or brass but will not affect the quality of the food. Iron, on the other hand, will discolor those foods so as to give them a less appealing darkened appearance.

12. Tin should be washed in hot, soapy water and dried thoroughly. A very light coating of oil will keep it from rusting.

13. Be careful using pottery, old or new, on a table top. Some of it is very rough and will scratch. Sit it on a pad of towels or on a cutting board. Don't slide it on the table surface even when picking up. Raise it straight up to move.

14. Pick up china, glassware or pottery with both hands and never by a handle or lip. A tea pot or pitcher should be supported with one hand on the bottom of the object.

15. When seasoning iron or it is best to use rendered suet. Order a chunk from your local market, cut it into small pieces and place in a heavy pan over low heat. Strain it and use the hot lard. Set the item you need to season in a large jelly roll type pan and coat the inside. Put it in the oven at 150 degrees and leave it for 2 hours. Remove the pan (be very careful—it will be extremely hot), turn the pan over and repeat the process with the outside of the pan. After the second 2 hours remove the pan from the oven, let it cool and then wash it with warm, soapy water. Rinse and re-

turn to the oven to dry. Don't use cooking oil to season. It leaves a sticky residue that is hard to remove.

16. Never lift an iron kettle or spider and sit it on a table top—even if you think the table has been protected. It doesn't take a lot of heat to permanently damage a table top. If the pan is extremely hot it could even cause a fire.

17. Old iron kettles are becoming scarce and generally when you find one someone has decided to use it for a planter and desecrated it with black spray paint. Heaven forbid! If you find one that is usable—no cracks and not chipped—there is one good way to restore it to usable condition. If you have a self cleaning oven (not a continuous clean) you can remove the paint or burned on crud simply by putting it in your oven, turned upside down, and cleaning the oven for a couple of hours. When the oven has turned off be very sure that the pan is cooled before removing it. Give it a good scrubbing and then season it according to the method described above. Presto! New pan.

SUBSTITUTIONS

½ Maple Sugar may be substituted for 1 cup of granulated sugar.

¾ cup of Maple Syrup may be substituted for 1 cup of granulated sugar.

(To substitute Maple Syrup for sugar in baking, use these same proportions but reduce the other liquid called for in the receipt by about 3 tablespoons for every cup of syrup substituted.)

One pint of Maple Syrup has the same sweetening power as 1 pound of Maple Sugar. To substitute, allow ½ cup for each cup of granulated sugar.

Molasses—is best in sweetening power if it replaces no more than ½ of the amount of sugar called for in the receipt. But in baking it is sometimes substituted—1 cup molasses for every cup of sugar. Add ½ teaspoon of soda for each cup added and omit the baking powder called for in the receipt (or use a small amount). Always reduce the other liquid by ¼ cup for each cup of molasses used.

Honey—In puddings, custards and pie fillings it is suggested that honey replace sugar cup for cup. As honey has almost twice the sweetness of sugar, this will greatly alter the flavor. Added to cake, cookies and bread dough, honey gives remarkable keeping qualities as well as a chewy texture.

In baking breads and rolls, 1 cup of honey can replace one cup of sugar. In cakes and cookies use ⅞ cup honey for 1 cup sugar. Be sure to reduce the liquid called for in the receipt by 3 tablespoons for every cup of honey. Unless sour milk or cream is called for in the receipt, add a mere pinch of baking soda—1/12 to 1/5 teaspoon.

When honey is used in jams, jellies and candies, a higher degree of heat must be used.

Yeast—To substitute dry granular yeast for compressed yeast, use 2 teaspoons of dry yeast granules to 2/3 ounce of cake yeast.

Sour Milk—Add 1 tablespoon vinegar or lemon juice to 1 cup of fresh milk. Pearlash is baking soda. Saleratus is cream of tartar.

Baking soda and cream of tartar mixed together become baking powder.

8 ounces cream of tartar and 6 ounces of baking soda: Use 1 teaspoon to each quart of flour being used.

(Modern: 2 teaspoons of cream of tartar plus 1 teaspoon bicarbonate of soda and 1/2 teaspoon salt for every cup of flour.)

Weights and Measurements

Flour and Sugar

3 1/2 cup unsifted whole wheat flour equals 1 pound
1 quart of white flour equals 1 pound
4 cups flour equals 1 pound
2 cups sugar equals 1 pound
1 cup granulated sugar is 8 ounces
1 cup confectioners sugar is 4 1/2 ounces
3 1/2 cup confectioners sugar equals 1 pound
1 cup brown sugar is 6 ounces
2 1/4 cups brown sugar is equal to 1 pound
4 pecks of flour equals one bushel
1 cup molasses or honey equals 12 ounces
1 cup of cornmeal is equal to 12 ounces
1 quart of cornmeal is 1 pound 1 ounces
1 quart maple sugar equals 2 3/4 pounds

> *"In the present age, indeed, cookery has been raised to the dignity of an art, and sages have given their treatises to the world."*
> —The Cook's Own Book, *by a Boston Housekeeper (Mrs. N.K.M. Lee), 1832*

Eggs
1 raw egg amounts to 3 tablespoons
10 raw eggs weighs 14-16 ounces, depending on size
10 raw eggs is equal to 1 pint or 1 pound

Weights & Measurements

Butter
½ pound equals 1 cup or ½ pint
¼ pound is ½ cup
1 tablespoon equals ½ ounce
1 teaspoon is ⅙ of an ounce

Butter the size of:

Filbert = 1 teaspoon, rounded
Hazelnut = 1 teaspoon, rounded
Butternut = 1 dessert spoon, rounded
Walnut = 1 tablespoon
Pullet's egg = 1½ ounces
Hen's egg = 2 ounces

Butter, when soft, is 1 pound or 1 quart.

Spices

1 ounce powdered allspice = 4½ tablespoons
1 ounce powdered cloves = 4 tablespoons
1 ounce powdered nutmeg = 3½ tablespoons
1 ounce powdered ginger = 5 tablespoons
1 ounce ground pepper = 3½ tablespoons
1 ounce table salt = 2 tablespoons
1 ounce powdered sage = 3 tablespoons
3 ounce chopped parsley = 16 tablespoons
1 ounce grated chocolate = ¼ cup

"We must eat to live and live to eat."
—Henry Fielding, 1707-1754

General Weights & Measurements

3/8 cup = 1/4 cup + 2 tablespoons
5/8 cup = 1/2 cup + 2 tablespoons
7/8 cup = 3/4 cup + 2 tablespoons
1 cup = 1/2 pint or 8 fluid ounces or 16 tablespoons
2 cups = 1 pint
2 cups water = 1 pound
1 quart, liquid = 2 pints
1 gallon, liquid = 4 quarts
1 tablespoon = 1/2 ounce
1 penny weight = 1/20 ounce
1 drachm = 1/8 ounce
1 small pinch = 1/6 teaspoon
1 large pinch = 1/8 teaspoon
1 salt spoon = 1/4 teaspoon
4 salt spoons = 1 teaspoon
3 teaspoons = 1 tablespoon
1 dessert spoon = 2 teaspoons
4 tablespoons = 1/2 cup or 2 ounces
5 1/3 tablespoons = 1/3 cup or 16 teaspoons
16 tablespoons = 1 cup or 8 ounces
1 cup = 1/2 pint
1 small coffee cup = 3/4 cup
1 large teacup = 1 cup
1 small teacup = 1/2 cup or 4 ounces or 8 tablespoons
1 wine glass = 1/4 cup or 4 tablespoons
1 tumbler = 1 cup
1 pint = 1/2 quart or 2 cups
4 quarts = 1 gallon
1 ounce liquid = 2 tablespoons
4 gills = 2 cups or 1 pint or 1/2 quart
2 gills = 1 cup or 1/2 pint
1 gill = 1/2 cup or 1/4 pint or 4 fluid ounces or 8 large tablespoons

COOKING ON THE HEARTH

General Information & Explanations

Firewood—Most any wood, cut trees or scrap wood, will burn but not all wood will produce a good cooking fire. The best cooking woods generate an intense, even heat and produce sufficient redhot coals. Hardwoods will give the coals needed but extra care must be taken that these woods be seasoned (aged), well dried but not so much as to be pithy. In Indiana, the best available woods are ash, beech, birch, hickory, oak, maple, cherry and walnut.

To secure coals for the hearth the fire must rest on andirons so the coals are allowed to drop to the floor of the fireplace. The coals are gathered with the use of an ash shovel and placed on the hearth. The spider or dutch oven is set on top of the coals, the food is put into the pan, the lid placed on top and then coals are placed on the lid.

To Adjust the Amount of Heat—If a pot that is hanging on the crane over the fire is getting too much heat, simply move the pot along the crane until it is not getting direct heat or swing it out and away from the fire. On the hearth, if food is cooking or baking too rapidly, reduce the amount of coals under and on top of the baking pan.

Temperatures
300 degrees = Slow or "Afternoon" Oven
350 to 375 degrees = Moderate Oven
400 to 425 degrees = Hot Oven
450 to 475 degrees = Very Hot or Quick Oven

Large or Great Spoonsful = Tablespoon

Turks Head Mold = Modern Bundt Pan

Pastry Jig = Pie Crimper

"Neats Tongue" = Beef tongue

Rosewater = Water distilled from rose petals. Not readily available. Substitute an equal amount of vanilla extract.

Potash = Obtained by leaching wood ashes and evaporating the lye. The residue yields crude potash. Purified potash, a white solid, is often called Pearlash.

INDEX OF RECIPES BY HOUSE

INDEX OF RECIPES BY HOUSE

The Fenton House:

The Baker House:

The Curtis House:

Salt-glazed pottery pieces such as these crocks and pitchers made at Conner Prairie's Baker house, were an indispensable part of pioneer life.

Lids were dried before being fired. They covered crocks of milk, kraut, pickles or preserves.

About the Editor

Margaret Hoffman, a fifth generation Hoosier, was born and raised in Hammond, Indiana. Married in 1945 to George B. Hoffman Jr., Margaret and her husband moved to Carmel, Indiana in 1969 after George was elected to the office of judge on Indiana's Court of Appeals.

Margaret began working at Conner Prairie as an interpreter in 1974 after her five sons were raised. She later served as foodways coordinator for several years, researching early Hoosier "receipts" (or recipes) and training interpreters in the techniques of fireplace cooking. She also has taught hearthside cooking classes at Conner Prairie and elsewhere.

Presently Margaret enjoys cooking for her children and grandchildren in her own fireplace and beehive oven. She also designs patterns and teaches traditional early American folk crafts such as rug hooking, smocking, sewing, tailoring and stenciling/theoreom painting.